FINDING THE LOST ART OF EMPATHY

Connecting Human to Human in a Disconnected World

TRACY WILDE

HOWARD BOOKS
AN IMPRINT OF SIMON & SCHUSTER, INC.

NEW YORK NASHVILLE LONDON TORONTO SYDNEY NEW DELHI

Howard Books
An Imprint of Simon & Schuster, Inc.
1230 Avenue of the Americas
New York, NY 10020

Copyright © 2017 by Tracy Wilde

First Howard Books hardcover edition May 2017

HOWARD and colophon are trademarks of Simon & Schuster, Inc.

For information about special discounts for bulk purchases, please contact Simon & Schuster Special Sales at 1-866-506-1949 or business@simonandschuster.com.

The Simon & Schuster Speakers Bureau can bring authors to your live event. For more information or to book an event, contact the Simon & Schuster Speakers Bureau at 1-866-248-3049 or visit our website at www.simonspeakers.com.

Manufactured in the United States of America

10   9   8   7   6   5   4   3   2   1

Library of Congress Control Number: 2016051809

ISBN 978-1-5011-5629-8
ISBN 978-1-5011-5630-4 (ebook)

For Tennyson—because of you, I found empathy.
Forever grateful for your life.

To my brother, Krist—the most meaningful
voice in my life and the greatest example
of one who lives out this generous and wild empathy.

CONTENTS

FOREWORD

by Judah Smith

Tracy and I are cousins, so we have a long history together. And by "history," I mean a lot of great memories with an occasional family drama thrown in. In retrospect, I might have been the source of much of the drama. I've always had a flair for the dramatic. Anyway, many of my favorite childhood memories involve my cousins. We played together, we laughed together, we fought together, we spent holidays and vacations together.

I remember one holiday when I was eleven years old. It was winter, and several of us cousins had been playing together outside in the snow. We were heading back to the house when I slipped and fell flat on my back. Hard. I was sure I heard my spine snap or a rib break. I instantly started yelling, "I can't move anything! I broke my back, guys! It hurts so bad!" As I said, I've always been dramatic.

I was certain I was on the verge of death or at least suffering from a punctured lung, but my cousins didn't seem to share my concern. As a matter of fact, I specifically remember Tracy laughing. "Judah, you're fine. Just get up."

I refused. I lay on the driveway, whimpering pathetically, certain the chill I felt was the icy breath of death. It didn't occur to me at the time that I was lying in snow.

Finally, I told one of my cousins to find my mom and to tell her my back was broken and I needed her to come. Five minutes later, he came back—without my mom. He had a message from her, though: "Tell Judah his back isn't broken and to get up." Welcome to my childhood.

So I got up. And of course, my back was fine.

My point here is not that Tracy laughed at me (and then wrote a book about empathy twenty-five years later . . . oh, the irony). The point is that we all find ourselves flat on our backs at times. And in most cases, the circumstances are much more real than my imagined paralysis. In moments like those, being surrounded by friends who know about you, care about you, and stand beside you is essential.

I experienced this firsthand a few years ago when my father passed away from cancer. The initial months after his passing were the darkest of my life. I discovered the force and fury of true grief. I walked unwitting and unprepared into storms greater than any I've ever faced. Storms of doubt. Storms of discouragement. Storms of depression. It was a dark time for my soul, and it took longer than I could have imagined to find peace and stability again.

As I look back on my journey of grief and healing, two things stand out. First, God's unconditional grace sustained me every step of the way. I can't claim to have always been aware of it or to have appreciated it, but he led me, he held me, and he healed me.

Second, I was surrounded by the right people. Some were family, some were friends, some were leaders in our church, some were professional counselors. They had different approaches and different roles, but they shared one thing: true empathy. They knew me and they loved me, just as I was. No matter what I was going through. And no matter how long it took.

These people quite literally saved my life. Not with their words or counsel, helpful though that might have been. They saved me with love. They unconditionally stood with me, often silent, often weeping, as my soul found its way through the unfamiliar labyrinth of grief.

Empathy might be one of the truest qualities of authentic relationships. Empathy isn't about giving advice or shouting criticism from the outside. Anyone can do that. Empathy is about standing shoulder to shoulder with a friend, facing life together. It's about taking the time to walk a mile in his or her moccasins. It's about weeping with those who weep, laughing with those who laugh.

Here's the problem, though: I've discovered I'm better at receiving empathy than giving it. Much better. And I'm guessing you can relate. In this fast-paced and results-oriented world, empathy often goes underrated and uncelebrated. We tend to value empathy when we need it and when we receive it, but we too easily forget to show it to others. It takes effort and intentionality to see beyond ourselves and to voluntarily feel what others are feeling.

That is why this book is so timely and compelling. *Finding the Lost Art of Empathy* presents a clear, insightful portrait of the kind of friend we all value—and the kind of friend we want to become. Tracy defines God's empathy toward us, which finds its greatest expression in Jesus. She describes how that empathy flows through us to those around us. And finally, she demonstrates what this human-to-human connection can produce in our relationships.

Without a doubt, this book will produce positive change in your heart and in your friendships. You will find yourself more aware of those around you; you will be quicker to hear, slower to speak, and slower to judge.

I can't promise it will always be comfortable. Quite the opposite, actually. Empathy is risky, as Tracy points out. But once you experience the results of this kind of love, compassion, and concern—once you rediscover the lost art of empathy—you'll never go back.

INTRODUCTION

Eight years ago, I stood in the middle of a Barnes & Noble store with my face in my hands and cried uncontrollably. I felt completely humiliated for breaking down in a public place. When I went there, I thought I could at least control when and where I completely lost it. But I had no control. I was heartbroken, confused, embarrassed, and desperate for answers. This was one of the few outings I had attempted (by myself) since the death of Tennyson. We had planned to marry that coming May.

It had been almost a year since we met. One weekend, I got suckered into being a driver for a youth conference our church was hosting. It was supposed to be my day off, but I was one of the few people who could rent a car since I was over the age of twenty-five (and being the pastor's kid, these are the kinds of things you get volunteered for whether you want to or not). So I found myself racing back and forth on a cold winter day between the airport and the conference center, picking up featured speakers and musicians and then driving them back to the conference center. I'll admit that I was a bit annoyed that I found myself playing taxi driver instead of eating cereal in my pajamas. The idea of doing literally anything else sounded pretty awesome.

However, thankfully, my sister, Rachelle, was my copilot throughout the day. She's two and a half years older than me and my built-in best friend for life. She and her husband, Mark, had been married for just over a year, so it was fun to have some one-on-one time with her again. We worked out a pretty efficient system. I would drive, and she would go inside the airport to locate the individuals we were sent to pick up. On one of the trips, Rachelle rushed back to the car and said, "One of the guys is single and cute. Look pretty!" Rachelle was right. The single one was cute and charming and very intent on talking to me on our way to the conference center. He was tall, confident, kind, and loved God—all the things I wanted and considered in a possible husband. And after eight months of dating, we had the ultimate DTR (define the relationship). Yep, we finally had the marriage talk in a sandwich shop in Washington, DC, on a perfect sunny Friday afternoon in October.

Tennyson looked at me with his signature smile and told me he wanted to marry me, and I said I wanted to marry him too. He wasn't proposing but was trying to figure out logistics and schedules. A little unromantic, sure, but we both lived busy lives and lived in different places. I was commuting between my home in Boise, Idaho, and work in Washington, DC, and he lived in Boulder, Colorado, and traveled extensively for ministry. So after a bit of schedule shuffling, we decided May of the next year (just seven months away) would be the best month to get married. He said we would look at rings when I visited him and his family for Thanksgiving. This made me rather certain he would propose over Christmas while he was visiting me and my family. We left the sandwich shop, and I drove him to the airport and said good-bye. I didn't know it would be the last time I would see him.

Maybe it's in retrospect, but I drove away with the strangest feeling. The first man I ever said I loved just told me he wanted to marry me, and I knew that when he asked, I would say yes. But deep down I had a nagging and sick feeling that we were never going to get married.

Four days later, my nagging feelings became reality. Tennyson suddenly went missing. Friends and family couldn't find him, his phone kept going straight to voice mail, and text messages were never returned. My worst fears were realized when his body was found in the Rocky Mountains a few days later. I was devastated. I was left with a broken heart and so many unanswered questions—answers I still haven't found and may never get.

When I got the bad news, the weather every day that followed was cloudy, dark, and scary—an accurate reflection of how I felt.

The days and weeks that followed also brought sudden and uncontrollable outbursts of tears, just like in Barnes & Noble. Then I experienced my first panic attack. Until then I had never struggled with fear or anxiety. When it hit, I was sitting in a crowded Starbucks, and the room quickly began to close in on me. Every person around me was spinning or blurry. My heart started racing and beating so hard and fast that I thought it was going to beat out of my chest. My entire body began to sweat. I wanted to run away, but I was paralyzed by fear and couldn't move or speak. I felt as though I was trapped and suffocating in my own body with no escape. I thought I was going to die. *Terrifying* doesn't even begin to describe the experience. Even worse, it was the first of more to come. Every day I was full of fear, not knowing when and where another episode would strike again.

Between the random and unannounced panic attacks and the unexpected and uncontrollable outburst of tears, I rarely felt safe leaving the house alone, if at all. But there I was in a bookstore trying to find a book to help me. Books and words have always been a source of security and guidance for me. When I wanted to learn to knit, I got a book on knitting. When I wanted to learn more about a person of significance, I read the person's biography or autobiography. And now, I was grieving and feeling alone and displaced in the very place I normally felt at home. All I wanted was something to relate to—someone or something to connect with.

I needed something to tell me how to stop feeling terrible.

I needed something to tell me how to get better.

I needed something to hold on to.

I just needed a book.

I didn't know how to open my Bible anymore, the book I had held fast to all my life. The book that had always guided me. I was scared and alone and knew the ancient words of the text would tell me something I didn't want to hear in this moment: *God is sovereign still.* In that moment I just wanted a book that told me how to stop hurting.

Surely Barnes & Noble would have a book to help a woman who told the man she loved on a Friday that she would marry him and the following Tuesday he was gone. Right?

With makeup-clouded tears streaming down my face and staining my shirt and my broken heart on display, I quietly but fervently whispered to myself, "One day, when I get through this, I'm going to write a book to help people who are hurting not to feel so alone."

We have all been that woman crying in Barnes & Noble. We have all felt alone, scared, and desperate for answers.

However, in that moment I didn't *feel* relatable. I felt alone. I felt isolated. I felt invisible. I felt like everyone was busy living their happy, easy, and content lives, but as I looked around, I noticed something: the people around me who looked so busy and preoccupied—they were looking at their phones or wearing headphones as they walked around the store—might be hurting too. Everyone has a story. Everyone has had deep moments of pain and tragedy.

I started looking at faces and realized that we don't really look at each other—maybe because we're too focused on getting in and getting out of places. Maybe it's because it's a socially awkward thing to do. But when we don't look at each other, we don't know who might be hurting and could use a smile or a hello (unless, of course, they are crying uncontrollably like I was). We rarely know what kind of day a person is really having—something we could quickly determine if we simply looked. The saddest part is that we often don't even care to know. It's no secret we live among pain. Divorce happens all too often. Death comes before we are prepared to say good-bye to a loved one. Sickness unfairly inflicts bodies. Disappointments are inevitable—this is why we need one another. We need people who care. We need empathy.

I've come a long way since the public panic attacks and uncontrollable sobs in random establishments. I moved through grief and let grief move through me. I embraced the process and its stages and allowed it to shape me into a person who sees and hears others more clearly, loves more freely, and forgives more easily. Struggles have a way of doing that for us if we let them. Traversing through life's treacherous paths gives us a lens to see the world through, a lens shaped by empathy. Tennyson's life and death taught me that. He taught me that people matter more than my perspective and opinions. What other people think, feel, and say matters. Empathy matters. It's not that I didn't love people before, but I didn't really see and hear them as I do now. Now, I'll be the first one to run into the battlefield with you. I'll be the last one to leave your side.

That's the power of empathy.

It gives us the ability to see from someone else's perspective and hear and understand that person's story in a new way. It becomes more about others than it is about self. I'm not perfect at it yet, but I'm committed to it. I've discovered some tools that have helped me journey down a more empathetic path as well as some barriers that try to keep me from walking in empathy. I think back to that moment in the bookstore and constantly try to give people what I wanted most in that moment. I try not to get caught up in my own actions and transactions and instead look at the people around me.

However, the first barrier we all must overcome is self.

We are a self-obsessed culture. It's not hard to find the evidence. Take a look at your TV, computer, phone, or even current song lyrics. We are so preoccupied with ourselves that we don't even seem to have the mental capacity to think about anyone else's feelings, happiness, or difficult circumstances. We dominate conversations rather than ask probing questions. We refresh our Instagram throughout the day but don't take time to look up and say hello to a neighbor, much less a stranger. And smartphones now have a category in their camera roll designated for all your selfies! Self-obsession seems to have become a pathological condition. And sadly, because we're so self-focused, we have lost the art of showing empathy. We've lost the ability to even notice that someone is hurting and could use a kind look, a touch, a hug, or words of comfort.

• • •

So, how is it that we hardly see one another anymore? What can we do to be less isolated and self-focused? How can we find ourselves without being absorbed with self? What are we afraid of when it comes to human connectedness? If God made us to be relational, why do we often avoid contact with others? What is the root problem of our bent toward isolation, and what is the solution?

These are a few of the questions I've asked myself since that day in Barnes & Noble and have subsequently tried to find the answers. In my search for deeper understanding, I have come to one conclusion: the root answer begins with losing yourself. Lose the self. Lose the selfies. Lose your life. Simple? Not even a little bit! This concept has been a problem since the beginning of time, and it has gotten worse. Jesus spoke to the human condition of self-obsession when he instructed his disciples to "lose" their lives: "For whoever would save his life will lose it, but whoever loses his life for my sake and the gospel will save it" (Mark 8:35). Over two thousand years later, we're all still working on this.

What does it mean to lose your life? It is to live beyond yourself. It's the antidote to self.

How do you lose your life? We must unself ourselves. The human condition is at its best and has potential for flourishing only when it turns away from self and lives in community with God and others.

So, back to Barnes & Noble.

I felt desperately alone. I wanted—no, needed—a book or a person to connect with. I needed someone to truly hear me and understand. I didn't want fluffy answers to the difficult questions in my heart or meaningless words to fill a void. Maybe I didn't need a book at all. Maybe I just needed love. Needed to be surrounded. Needed to know I wasn't alone. I needed empathy.

Through my journey of becoming a pastor, I've learned that a much simpler lifestyle is buried under thousands of years of cultures, with a much slower pace of living and a compassionate church from which Jesus, the supreme example, displayed what is now the lost art of empathy. It is an art so incredibly astounding that it could end wars and connect nations. It could save families from ruin. It could save couples from divorce. And it could help a brokenhearted girl, bawling her eyes out in a bookstore, find comfort and relief.

This book is an effort to rediscover the lost art of empathy.

I hope and pray that as a result of reading these pages, you will imagine and dream with me about a world filled with empathy. A place where shame and embarrassment don't exist, forgiveness freely flows, love and care for one another is as steady and natural as the air we breathe. A world where the hurting can heal, the broken can mend, and the lost can find home. Sounds a lot like heaven coming down, doesn't it? That's because it is. This is why Jesus taught the disciples to pray in Matthew 6:10 (NIV), he said,

"Your kingdom come, your will be done on earth as it is in heaven." He also said in Matthew 22:39 (ESV) to "love your neighbor as yourself." In a world that's known for self, let's be the agents of change and transform the narrative of self and make our lives and this world about reflecting heaven and loving our neighbor.

CHAPTER 1

Sympathy versus Empathy

*Courage is what it takes to stand up and speak; courage is
also what it takes to sit down and listen.*

—WINSTON CHURCHILL

I say, "I love you," to everyone.

I say, "I love you," to my family. I say, "I love you," to my
friends. I say, "I love you," to my neighbor Marilee. I say, "I
love you," to people I've just met. I say, "I love you," to my
dog. Most important, I say, "I love you," to baristas because
they give me coffee.

I freely say "I love you" because I love people. But it can
get weird.

The other day when I was at a meeting, I noticed a man I
didn't recognize wave to me from across the room with a big
smile, leading me to believe that I knew him. But I didn't
that I could remember. So as I walked across the room, I
dug deep into the recesses of my mind to recall who the guy
is and how I know this smiling stranger.

By the time I approach him, I've got nothing.

I don't know if he's from my church. I don't know if he works at my dry cleaners. I don't know if he's my fifth-grade teacher. All I know is he's still smiling and seems to know who I am.

So naturally, as that distance between us grows smaller and being a naturally loving person, I go in for the awkward hug. After the uncomfortable embrace, made more uncomfortable by my nerve-induced sweat, he makes a formal introduction, and I realize I didn't recognize him because I didn't know him!

Given my propensity for loving people in general, I'll probably always love and hug friendly strangers. But the reality is that there is a difference between loving a stranger or an acquaintance and showing love toward someone you know.

Think about the starting point of any relationship. It can start off really awkward, but then you get to know the person—you know their favorite food, how many siblings they have, where they're from, whether they are an INTJ or an ENFP (by the way, I'm an ESFJ). Obviously the level of your love for someone will develop and grow deeper the more you get to know that person. My love for the smiling stranger came from my overall love for people—for God's children. But my sister? Of course, my love for her runs far deeper.

There is a similar difference between sympathy and empathy.

When you sympathize with someone, you go online or to a store and peruse the sympathy cards. You usually find an array of visuals ranging from elegant-looking lilies to mopeyeyed puppies. You grab one, write "With love" and sign your name, seal and stamp it, and stick it in the mailbox.

Easy enough.

But when you show empathy, you step into a much deeper level of another person's pain. You jump in the pit and get your hands dirty. This can be done in a number of ways, and there are no limits. You can go to the hospital and sit with someone who is waiting to receive the good or bad news. You listen and attempt to understand the breadth of the situation, no matter how troubling or difficult. You're physically and emotionally available for whatever the need is at the time.

It's not so easy.

And it's where so many of us walk on by.

In my research to understand the difference between sympathy and empathy, I went back to the root of each word. For instance, *sympathy* comes from the Greek origin *sun*, meaning with, plus *pathos*, meaning feeling. So *sympathy* means with feeling.

On the flip side, empathy is *em*, meaning in, plus *pathos*, meaning feeling. *In* feeling. In the situation. In the valley with another hurting soul.

In a nutshell, sympathy skims the surface. That's not a bad thing; it's appropriate to show sympathy some of the time. But empathy goes deeper: it includes action. The key difference between the two is that the former can be shown without full understanding or connection.

Sympathy feels a lot like signing a card *with* love or giving a sweaty hug to a stranger.

Empathy is a whole lot more. It feels like being in feeling.

It feels (kind of) like being in love.

Walk a Mile

Please bear with me a moment while I attempt to get a little scientific on you. Keep in mind that I am by no means an expert (my only C in college was in biology), but I am an answer-seeking and research-collecting kind of woman, and I will indulge here.

Recent work in neuroscience has unlocked tremendous findings about empathy and the human brain. In one of philosophy's most famous and long-standing texts, *Leviathan*, Thomas Hobbes wrote that we humans are wired as self-interested creatures who seek only our own individual desires and needs. This philosophy of self-interest has certainly dominated our Western thinking. However, there is proof that we are also wired for empathy.

The discovery came from a team of neuroscientists at the University of Parma, Italy, in 1990. Italian researcher Giacomo Rizzolatti and his team (Luciano Fadiga, Vittorio Gallese, and Leonardo Fogassi) conducted experiments on monkeys with an implanted electrode in their brains. While observing the monkeys, the researchers discovered that a certain part of the monkey's brain, the premotor cortex, was activated when the monkey picked up an object. Later, they discovered quite inadvertently that the same part of the monkey's brain was activated and lit up when the monkey saw one of the researchers picking up that same object. Roman Krznaric, a social philosopher and leading voice on empathy, notes in his book *Empathy Why It Matters, and How to Get It* that this finding was later confirmed through more experiments with monkeys and humans by using functional magnetic resonance imaging (fMRI).* We've all experienced this phenomenon when we see someone stub his or her toe and we wince in pain as if we too had stubbed our toe.

Krznaric explains this groundbreaking evidence:

They had accidentally discovered "mirror neurons." These are neurons that fire up both when we experience something (such as pain) and also when we see somebody else going through the same experience. People with lots of mirror cells tend to be more empathetic, especially in terms of sharing emotions. According to Rizzolatti, "mirror neurons allow us to grasp the minds of others not through conceptual reasoning but through direct stimulation." Eminent neuroscientist Vilanyanur Ramachandran has compared the discovery of mirror neurons to Crick and Watson's

---

* Roman Krznaric, *Empathy: Why It Matters, and How to Get It* (New York: Penguin Random House, 2014), 21.

double-helix revelation: "I predict that mirror neurons will
do for psychology what DNA did for biology."*

If nothing else, this discovery of mirror neurons finally helps me solve the mystery as to why I yawn every time I see another person yawn: it is because of my empathetic brain! So we are actually wired for empathy. Great news! But if we are wired for it, then why don't we respond to our empathetic impulses? Well, mirror neurons are only part of the story.

We might be wired for empathy, but our brains aren't always activated for it.

Jeremy Rifkin, an American social theorist, shows in his book *The Empathetic Civilization* that although we have the ability for emotional empathy, which is fired by our mirror neurons, there is another side to our empathetic brain, which is our cognitive empathy. This is the aspect of empathy that helps us to understand not just the feelings of others but their thoughts as well. Cognitive empathy is putting yourself in someone's else place or perspective.

Rifkin argues that when this cognitive part of empathy is practiced,

one develops a moral sensitivity to the extent one is em-
bedded, from infancy, in a nurturing parental, familial,

---

*   Ibid., 21–22.

*and neighborhood environment. Society can foster that environment by providing the appropriate social and public context. While primitive empathic potential is wired into the brain chemistry of some mammals, and especially the primates, its mature expression in humans requires learning and practice and a conducive environment.**

In other words, we can train ourselves to be more empathetic by putting ourselves in an emotionally neutral state and then letting our neutral emotions enter into another person's pain and think from his or her perspective. Strictly speaking, we can become more empathetic by training ourselves to think about a situation from our own point of view *and* from someone else's. The problem is that we often struggle to make this brain connection due to the fact that we rely on our own thoughts and feelings as a reference for viewing others rather than a neutral state. I call this the Thomas Hobbes effect. Simply put, we don't know how to put ourselves in another person's world. We rely on our own feelings, self-interests, and experiences to be our gauge for empathy. For example, if you have spent the holidays with your entire extended family, you have a pretty good gauge on your empathy scale when you take

---

* Jeremy Rifkin, *The Empathetic Civilization: The Race to Global Consciousness in a World in Crisis* (New York: Penguin, 2009), 177.

a look at blending family traditions. As we get older and start our own families, we also begin new traditions and preferences, and they often look drastically different from those of our other family members. Instead of recognizing how foolish it is to be obsessed with our self-interest and traditions, we often explode with anger and frustration at our loved ones because one person wants to open presents Christmas Eve while the other person wants to open them Christmas morning.

Sound ridiculous?

Lack of empathy often is.

Our brain wants to work to adjust and correct our self-centered tendencies, but we have to practice thinking from a perspective different from our own.

Neuroscientists believe our brains are extremely malleable. A significant amount of research concludes that the ability to show empathy can improve greatly with practice. If this is true, then this is great news for all of us! We don't have to have shared experiences (or been through what others have been through) in order to empathize with another person; we just need to practice placing ourselves in another person's world.[*]

You no doubt know the often-heard adage that says, "You can't really understand another person's experience until you've walked *a mile in their shoes*." I think a better

---

[*] Krznaric, *Empathy*, 27.

approach to empathy is to *put ourselves in another person's world*. When you place yourself in another person's world, you see and experience his perspective from his point of view (i.e., cultural context and historiocity as well as linguistic nuances). When we do this, we can better experience the scope of his feelings and life. By putting ourselves in the midst of his world, consistent and intentional empathy can become habitual and second nature to us.

Aristotle was right: "We are what we repeatedly do; excellence, then, is not an act but a habit." Practice makes perfect. Training ourselves to think and feel what another person might be experiencing *is* possible. In fact, it is the best way to be human. The more we do something, the more it becomes who we are. The exciting part of this concept is that it applies to everyone. None of us are too far from loving our neighbor and living an altruistic life. None of us are too far from putting ourselves in another person's world. All of us are on the journey together, learning to be present and to listen.

We practice ways to succeed in our careers, education, or finances. We measure our success by who we know, what kind of car we drive, and the price tag on our clothes. We rarely think of empathy as a measure of success. I think the most successful people in the world are the ones who can recognize a need and activate empathy in the midst of our growing self-obsessed world.

So, good news! Getting an A in empathy is way more important than getting a C in biology (at least that's what I tell myself).

Active Listening

Recently I was at church listening to a message by a preacher who was giving a practical and personal illustration to the scripture he was highlighting. I had stayed up a little too late the night before and hadn't yet had enough coffee to fully engage like I usually do, but I laughed when everyone else laughed, said "amen" when others around me shared the sentiment, and even wrote notes (well, doodled on my notepad).

Out of the blue, the preacher must have said something quite funny because the congregation roared in laughter. Naturally I joined in and even added a hand-to-knee slap. My friend sitting next to me said, "What did he say? I missed it." Busted! I had no idea what the preacher said because I clearly wasn't listening and neither was my friend. So while everyone was connected to the preacher and his illustration, my friend and I were completely out of the loop.

I was immediately convicted when I thought back on my seminary years when I had studied the concept of active listening. Active listening is not easy. Essentially it is the ability to be totally present in the moment. It requires our full attention and the ability to shut our brain off and stop thinking about anything except for what another person is saying. That's hard. The entire point of active listening is to listen to gain understanding. It requires that the listener ask questions in the quest to comprehend. The listener will seek to confirm she is on the right track by responding,

"This is what I hear you saying." It's to help verify that the listener truly is on the path to understanding.

However, most of the time when we're listening to someone, our brains are working hard to process the next thing *we're* going to say. We tend to listen to respond, not to understand. How many conversations have you had where someone was pouring out her heart to you, and you were thinking and formulating what you were going to say the moment there was a break in her speech? We do this all the time! But you can't effectively listen to someone if you're thinking about what you're going to say when she finally stops talking. How many times have you looked down at your phone because you felt uncomfortable with the person or crowd you were with, or because you felt the awkwardness that comes with being alone? Or what about when sitting at stoplights? Or at dinner parties (when you should be engaging in the conversation)? Sitting in a coffee shop? We all do it.

But what if we were more intentional?

What if we were more willing to engage?

What if we sought strangers out for conversation?

Jesus illustrates this for us in John 4 when he engages in conversation with a woman at a well. It was a dialogue with a Samaritan woman—one who, culturally and historically, had no voice or status in society. He positioned himself to have a conversation with someone no one else would have dared talk to. It was the sixth hour of the day, which was considered a very unusual time to come to a well in ancient times. This indicated that those who came at that hour didn't want to be seen or talk to others. And yet Jesus sat down by the well and waited. When the woman approached, he asked for a drink in order to start a conversation. This wasn't a chance encounter: Jesus had placed himself there. He knew she was struggling and searching for love in all the wrong places. She had been married four times and was now sleeping with a man who wasn't her husband. But instead of avoiding the topic and a potentially compromising situation—a man couldn't be seen talking to a woman alone—Jesus stayed and conversed. He acknowledged her circumstances without judgment and gave her hope for a new and different kind of life.

Jesus models for us something the rest of us struggle to exercise. He didn't try to avoid an uncomfortable conversation; rather, he strategically placed himself in a situation where he could give complete attention to the woman even though he broke every social taboo of his time.

Sadly, we have become a society of conflict avoiders. In other words, we're conversation dodgers when it comes to talking about painful and uncomfortable circumstances. One of the calls for every person is to be relational—it's the way we were intended to be—which involves uplifting, meaningful, and encouraging conversation, even with those whom we are taught to culturally evade.

Think about it. If we engage only with people who have the same socioeconomic status as us, how will we learn about and connect with people different from us? Just imagine if when we run into someone who we know is suffering, we stop to converse and engage about real-life issues, as Jesus did. Our capacity for empathy would grow, our perspective and sensitivity toward others would broaden, and our lives would look a lot more like Jesus'.

Text messaging and Facebook have become our replacement for human connection and conversation, so when an actual human sits down face-to-face and begins to talk, we struggle to know how to gauge that person's mood or carry on a meaningful conversation. We have an escape addiction to our media devices. You don't believe me? How many times have you had to stop reading this book to check your phone? If you get to a restaurant before the person you are meeting arrives, do you scroll through Instagram and Snapchat, or do you engage in conversation with someone around you, perhaps the waiter? Exactly. To be fair, I am every bit as guilty as the next person.

We can't have healthy or thriving relationships with people if we don't actively listen and engage with them . . . and I mean *really* listen.

I can have a conversation with someone and not *hear* a single thing she said to me. She can talk away, or even confess to a murder, while I think about that funny thing Jimmy Fallon said the night before on the *Tonight Show*, or make a mental list of all the things I need to accomplish in the next four hours. We're masters at this. We can smile and nod at the appropriate times and throw in the occasional "wow," "totally," "so sorry," or "yeah, for sure." We know how to have full conversations without ever hearing anything. And then we walk away feeling proud of ourselves for giving another human some of our precious time and day when actually we gave her nothing. In fact, it was less than nothing. We gave her the impression of empathic listening, but we gave only the illusion that we care. And that illusion is shallow and dehumanizing.

A boyfriend once gave me Gary Chapman's bestselling book, *The Five Love Languages: How to Express Heartfelt Commitment to Your Mate*. We were dating and he wanted me to know his love language (I got it—but that's another story). The book is excellent and has no doubt done wonders for relationships around the world. It also made the phrase "filling your love tank" famous.

Chapman argues that every person gives and receives love in the five categories he lays out in the book: gifts, quality time, words of affirmation, acts of service, and physical touch. The nature and premise is to teach couples to explore and discover (through the corresponding love language test) what their companion's love language is so they are better able to give love the way their partner best receives it. Rarely do couples share the same primary love language, which is why this book proved to be so helpful. Chapman's goal is to teach readers how to speak their loved one's love language—not their own. The book, groundbreaking when it was published in 1995, has evolved into more editions that include more than just romantic couples. There are now editions for singles, children, teenagers, those in the military, men, and women.

My number one love language is acts of service. If someone (say, my sweet sister-in-law, Kelly) comes over to my house and helps assemble the credenza I ordered for my dining room, I will turn into a big puddle of love. There's something about someone going out of his or her way to help me with something that melts my heart. Chapman's love language theory states that people should not use the language *they* like to receive but the language in which the other person best receives love.

The only way you can know someone's love language is by listening. For instance, if you hear your friend or spouse say something like, "I miss spending time with you," you can pretty much bank on quality time being her primary love language. Or perhaps a frustrated stay-at-home mom barks at her husband the moment he walks in the house after a long day, "I just wish I could get some help around here." Acts of service might be that exhausted mom/wife's love language. And the person who feels the need to constantly touch you for no apparent reason is probably trying to tell you that his language is physical touch. You can also tell someone's love language by observing how that person gives to others. If someone likes to give gifts, then gifting is likely the language she likes to receive. If someone is always giving others words of affirmation, that's likely his language since we typically speak our own language.

But this is where a lot of us get it wrong.

In order to connect with someone else, we must learn to speak that person's language, not ours.

The other day, my friend Kate told me she was trying to figure out a good way to reach out to a mutual friend who was going through a painful loss. Kate said with a sigh, "I'm just not good with words. So I stopped by her house, but she didn't seem to want my help with anything." What I remembered and realized in that moment was that our friend has a love language of words of affirmation, so that's what the hurting friend needed. Kate, who is a lot like me, offered acts of service, *not* what our friend needed. What she needed were *words*. This is where so many of us fall short in our efforts to show empathy. We reach out the way we think *we* would want to receive it instead of how the other person needs it.

So back to the benefits of active listening: they are twofold. On one end, you listen to gain perspective—neutralizing your thoughts and emotions, then putting yourself in the other person's world. The person on the other end receives the gift of truly being heard. Listening is at its best when we listen to understand, not to respond. That's when empathy reaches its fullest impact. If we could all grasp this one concept—listening to understand—I think we could change the world. At least we would change our

marriage, families, friendships, and work relationships—
not a bad thing to strive for.

Empathy Gap

My mom is the quintessential nurturing mom. She's the
greatest in all forms and ways. She is my biggest cheer-
leader, supporter, and encourager. And my mom loves to tell
her three kids how much she loves us and is proud of us (I
hope I inherited this trait). The only problem is that those
three kids, now grown and living on their own, don't exactly
like talking on the phone.

Mom's phone calls typically last longer than we want
even though we say, "Gotta run, Mom," or, "Sounds great;
I'll talk to you later." She, like any other great mom, finds
another extremely important talking point to delay the inevitable good-bye. So when our mom would call to have a chat
or check in with her adult kids, we would easily let it go to
voice mail. We had become text, not talk, people.

One day I was with my mom, and she noticed I was
texting. She asked who I was texting, and I told her it was
Krist, my older brother—her firstborn. In fact, it turned
out that she had been trying to reach Krist for hours, to
no avail. She turned to me and asked, "Will you teach me
how to text?" A little shocked, I looked at her and saw the
wheels turning in her head. In that moment, my smart
mom discovered she was going to have to start texting if she

hoped to stay connected to her kids as she liked. Of course I obliged, and now Mom is the queen of texting. And she must get her tech-savvy ways from her mom, because her mom, my ninety-five-year-old grandma, has an iPhone and an Instagram account!

Those of us born in the 1980s and 1990s have never known anything other than communicating through technology. This trend developed into a standard way of life right before our eyes and into our hands. I got my first cell phone when I was fifteen years old, a young age back then to have a cell phone (though not compared to today's standards). I was one of the few kids my age who had a cell phone. Even more incredible, my older brother and sister, respectively, four and two years older than me, didn't have their own cell phones yet.

I am a part of the first generation to grow up in the Information Age. It was great! Writing papers for school became far easier with the use of the Internet rather than having to spend hours in a library. My mom worried less about me when I was out late with friends because I could call her to let her know where I was. If I had car trouble or ran out of gas, it was no big deal and nothing to fear since I could use my phone to call AAA. Productivity, peace of mind, and safety were just a few of the many benefits of the rising digital age.

What we didn't realize as we were sending an email instead of having a face-to-face meeting or a text message instead of a coffee date is that we began losing the very thing that humans were created to do: converse and relate on a personal level. Making eye contact is now something I have to consciously think about doing. Listening is something I have to force myself to engage in. And yet these are the fundamental aspects of human connection.

We are now entering our second generation of users, so what started as a trend is now commonplace for everyone. What's more, my generation is now leading homes and communities—even our world. We are having children who are introduced to cell phones, computers, tablets, and remote controls when they are toddlers. We are now many of the decision makers on Capitol Hill and the influencers in Hollywood. Yet we have become inept at talking face-to-face with meaning and ease. I think this is a contributing factor to the rise of online dating. Twenty- and thirty-somethings are far more comfortable meeting a potential significant other online or using a dating app rather than face-to-face in a public setting.

Sherry Turkle, Abby Rockefeller Mauzé Professor of the Social Studies of Science and Technology at MIT, has spent the past thirty years studying and researching the psychology of people's relationships with technology. In her latest book, *Reclaiming Conversation: The Power of Talk in a Digital Age*, Turkle believes that much of the reason for this "crisis of empathy" in our culture today is due to our relationship with digital technology. In other words, our phones are creating an empathy gap.

Simply put, we don't know how to empathize because we don't know how to have face-to-face conversations. The way we develop emotional intelligence and the ability to read body language can occur only from live conversations. Turkle observes, "In the past twenty years we've seen a 40 percent decline in the markers for empathy among college students, most of it within the past ten years. It is a trend that researchers link to the new presence of digital communications."* Turkle's antidote to this growing problem is reclaiming conversation: learning how to engage with one another face-to-face, learning to listen, and learning to read body language. Without conversation we have become emotionally underdeveloped. (And, no, emojis don't count.) Because conversation growth has been stunted, particularly among millennials and those younger, it has seemed to develop rather emotionally immature adults. These adults can't handle face-to-face conflict with a coworker, a spouse, or a friend. The trend is to retreat rather than talk. Or just send a text message. Maybe unfriend or unfollow them on social media outlets to avoid them altogether. I used to believe that conflict avoidance was a personality trait, but I've come to believe it is more of a reflection of an underdeveloped social skill called communication.

Social awkwardness and anxiety have become a growing

---

* Sherry Turkle, *Reclaiming Conversation: The Power of Talk in a Digital Age* (New York: Penguin Press, 2015), 21.

epidemic. At any dinner party, you would be hard-pressed not to find a one-upper (you know this guy; for every story you tell, he has a bigger and better one), conflict avoider, passive-aggressive commenter, a know-it-all, and simply a nonlistener.

Here's the thing: technology is here to stay and will probably only increase in its cultural veracity. I'm thankful for the improvements technology has made, especially in spreading the gospel. Thanks to the Internet, I get to teach classes for a college in Kenya that trains and equips pastors all over that beautiful country. Thus far in my life, this is one of the most rewarding things I have been a part of. If it wasn't for the web, getting these pastors the resources they need or the ability for them to send me their papers and projects to be graded would take weeks rather than seconds.

I'm not here to tell you to throw your phones and computers away and move to the mountains of Idaho and live as mountain people (although if you've never been to Idaho, you don't know what you're missing). Rather, I'm suggesting we relearn how to engage with one another by listening, talking, and caring for others in spite of our growing trend toward disengagement. Perhaps we can use technology for efficiency rather than letting technology use us.

Empathy in Action

The first warm day of spring was begging me to go outside and enjoy it and inaugurate the budding flowers and bursts of sunshine by going for a run. I laced up my running shoes, grabbed my phone and earphones, and ran out the door. Not sure if I was wrapped up in a world of chirping birds or the feeling of the warm sun beating on my shoulders that I had missed for months, but all I know is I wasn't paying attention to the road I was running on and fell in a pothole. I managed to break my fall (not gracefully, I'm sure), but my phone went flying in the air, as if in slow motion, and landed face down on a rock. "Please, Lord. Please, Lord," was the only thing I could get out of my mouth as I walked over to pick up the phone and survey the damage. All you iPhone owners know the rest of this story. As I picked up the phone and turned it around . . . yep . . . shattered screen. I couldn't even touch the screen without shards of glass cutting my finger. A new phone was inevitable.

Two weeks later, I was leading a missions team to New York City. We had fed the homeless and worked all day in a warehouse store that gives away food, clothes, and other household items to people in need in the community. I was leading these young students all over New York on the subway and showing them the sights of the Big Apple. One afternoon I had put my new phone in my back pocket. When I went to use the restroom, I forgot where my phone was. Phone. Toilet. End of story. Another phone bites the dust.

A few weeks after my trip to New York (I am not making this up), I was enjoying a beautifully warm day in a boat on a lake doing what I love to do: wake-surf. If I could be a professional anything, I would want to be a professional wake surfer. It is my favorite hobby ever. All my friends on the boat that day were laughing, listening to music, and watching my brother-in-law wake-surf as I was capturing all the moments by videoing it on my phone, live for Periscope (Is that app still a thing?). Anyway, I was showing the world (I think I had maybe ten followers on Periscope) what a wonderful time my friends and I were having, when all of the sudden, the rope being used to pull the surfer to the boat hit my hand that was holding my phone. And plop. Water. Phone. Bye. There went my phone to the bottom of the Cascade Lake.

All three phones were goners. Thank goodness for insurance. (Always get the insurance for your phone.) Each time I sheepishly walked in the Apple Store to explain my embarrassing reasons for needing a new phone (the New York City toilet was the worst), the Apple employee always made me feel understood and seemed genuinely sorry for the inconvenience and was willing to help—even if it took four hours.

When Steve Jobs and Steve Wozniak started Apple in 1976 in Jobs's parents' garage, no one would have believed it would become one of the world's leading companies in technology. In the early 1980s, Mike Markkula, one of the first investors in Apple and a close acquaintance of Jobs, wrote a memo, "The Apple Marketing Philosophy," that is now considered the DNA of Apple. The first point in the memo was *empathy*. Markkula stressed the importance of understanding the needs and feelings of customers. "We will truly understand their needs better than any other company," he wrote.

This emphasis on empathy has continued over the many decades of Apple's success. And today the Genius Bar employees (like the ones who helped me three separate times with my phones) are taken through training. The *Genius Training Student Workbook* teaches each employee how to understand each customer's needs and how to make each person happy.*

The manual reiterates the word *empathy* over and over and encourages employees to implement the "three F's" ("feel, felt, and found") when identifying with a customer's need.

"I see how you *feel*."

"I would have *felt* the same way"

"I think I have *found* a solution."

What Apple is genius at (no pun intended) is recognizing and understanding how the customer feels right away. You are far more likely to keep swiping that credit card at a store that makes you feel understood.

Apple isn't the only company making empathy a part of its business philosophy. Ford Motor Company is also lead-

---

* Sam Biddle, *How to Be a Genius: This Is Apple's Secret Employee Training Manual* (2012), http://gizmodo.com/5938323/how-to-be-a-genius-this-is-apples-secret -employee-training-manual.

ing the way in exercising empathy. This is only fitting since founder Henry Ford once famously said, "If there is any one secret of success, it lies in the ability to get the other person's point of view and see things from that person's angle as well as from your own."

According to a recent article in the *Wall Street Journal*, many companies are recognizing the need for empathy and are implementing empathy training for their employees. CEOs and executives are learning the great need for listening to understand.

Ford Motor Company is one these companies. It started having its male engineers wear an "empathy belly" with a stimulator that mimics pregnancy symptoms such as bladder pressure, extra weight, and even back pain. They do all this with the hope that they can better understand the needs of this specific customer and how that can be reflected in the engineering of Ford automobiles. Ford has also done a similar experiment with "age suits" to better relate to the needs of aging customers, with such issues as blurry vision and stiff joints.* These practices have helped the engineers to understand the challenges some drivers experience. One of the changes that is believed to be influenced by empathy training has been easier automatic adjustments of the driver's seat.

If the corporate world is recognizing the need to exercise

---

* Joann S. Lublin, "Companies Try a New Strategy: Empathy Training," *Wall Street Journal*, June 21, 2016, http://www.wsj.com/articles/companies-try-a-new-strategy-empathy-1466501403.

empathy training, we should as well. What if we implemented empathy training in our own everyday, ordinary lives? We could just as easily implement Apple's three F's or Ford's Empathy Belly in our lives.

For some people, empathy is just more natural; for the rest of us, I'm very grateful that empathy can be partly trained.

P.S. I'm very happy and quite proud to report that I haven't had to get a new iPhone in well over a year now. Knock on wood. But if I did, I'm pretty confident that those Apple employees would show me some empathy.

CHAPTER 2

Andre Agassi

Everybody thinks of changing humanity and nobody thinks of changing himself.

—Leo Tolstoy

I think I raised a narcissist. My dog is fully convinced every human being is here to serve him, pet him, feed him, greet him, play with him—the list is endless. It's so embarrassing when I take him on a walk and he sees a person, a dog, a cat, or a bear (he's no respecter of species) coming and takes off full speed to greet them. Luckily he's cute and small so everyone thinks he's a puppy and thus happily greets and pets him. I blame myself and my parents, whom I share joint custody with . . . long story. Basically, I'm a terrible dog owner, and what grown-up child hasn't passed their dog onto their parents (or at least tried) at some point or another? Exactly.

In 2006, my favorite athlete of all time, Andre Agassi, retired. I had a poster of him on my wall growing up—he was wearing bright neon colors and had a long mane of hair. His eyes pierced my very soul. He was certainly my first celebrity crush. I refused to cheer for his rival, Pete Sampras, because I was eternally loyal to the bad boy of tennis. I grew up playing tennis because of Agassi and made sure to learn only a two-handed backhand just like my idol. (Recently I was teaching a class of twentysomething college students who had NO IDEA who Andre Agassi is. I have never felt older in my life.)

When Agassi retired in 2006, I coincidentally decided to get a dog the same month and I named him Andre Agassi Wilde. I can usually tell who the tennis fans are out there with their ability to pronounce *A-ga-see* correctly. My little Agassi was the puppy I always wanted. He is a ten-pound, black-haired, blue-eyed Maltese and poodle mix—a Maltipoo. I had never owned a dog by myself before. When I was growing up, we had one family dog: a yellow lab named Honey Popcorn Wilde. My brother, sister, and I were given the opportunity to choose between two beautiful little lab puppies, and of course we unanimously chose the hyper, bubbly, carefree pup who leaped into our arms and hearts rather than the shy, slow, less exciting pup who had to be helped out of the car by the breeder.

Honey lived up to her first impression and was a nonstop energetic pup. She chewed the entire backyard, knocked me over with her tail anytime I went outside (hence, I never went outside), and ran away from home so many times my mom has a criminal record due to her misdemeanor for "dog running at large." Eventually Honey got sent to live with a very nice family who had another dog with lots of space for her to run. Before you think our parents pulled a fast one on us . . . it's true Honey went to live with our aunt and uncle and cousins, so we got to see Honey the rest of her life and she was much happier with her new family.

So when I got Agassi, I had never owned or taken care of a dog before. I had no idea what I was getting myself into. Disclaimer: dear moms, do not crucify me for what I'm about to say . . . I realize puppies and babies are very different so just bear with me as I make a hyperbolic comparison. I'm embarrassed to admit this, but I'm pretty sure I had the puppy owner's version of postpartum depression after the first week. My new pup whined all night, I had to take him outside every two hours to go potty, he chewed half of the shoes in my shoe closet, and I had no life anymore because I couldn't leave him for more than a couple of hours. I wanted to send him back! I tried giving him away several times. We even attempted to gift him to my sister's in-laws.

My dog was nothing like what I expected. I was exhausted and not sure the dog life was fitting my lifestyle. It wasn't until I caved and started treating him like a human that things really improved. Since he whined and cried all night in his crate, I decided to let him sleep in bed with me, and it was like magic. He no longer needed to go outside so frequently. And since this new mommy lifestyle was cramping my style, I started bringing him everywhere I went, so I no longer felt trapped at home with no social life. It was great! He became my little buddy, my accessory. I even got one of those cute dog purses to carry him in while shopping or going to movies or restaurants. This new rhythm was working just fine until the day Agassi got treated like who he really was: a dog. I had trained Agassi to think he was human, so the moment he got into trouble for peeing in the house and sent to his crate for punishment, he looked at me in complete disgust and shock. He soon got too big for the purse, so instead of coming with me everywhere, he stayed locked in the laundry room until I returned. One time, to show his displeasure with this new arrangement, he looked straight into my eyes as we stood in the middle of my living room, lifted his leg, and peed while staring me down. Nine years later, there is all new flooring and furniture in my house, and Agassi is *still* working on acting more like a dog than a human.

Agassi was so used to being treated like a little human that he didn't know or understand what it meant to live like a dog. I think we humans do the same thing to a degree: We live as if the world revolves around us. We become conditioned to our comfortable settings and don't want to be bothered with change or inconvenience. In a world where we are at the center, it's easy to walk past or even over others.

Have you ever wondered why that husband and father of four babies could walk out on his family? Or why someone will refuse to listen to what anyone else has to say about a matter? Or why that woman can so heartlessly spread lies about you? Or how a family member could betray you for opportunity? The moment we believe, whether consciously or subconsciously, that we're more important than others—

that what we want supersedes the needs and desires of others—we open the door to live as unempathetic humans.

Let's be honest. If my dog were a human (and I don't mean the real Andre Agassi), psychologists would be quick to diagnose him as a classic textbook narcissist. One of the distinguishing characteristics of narcissism is the inability to have empathy for others. The sad reality is that with empathy becoming an increasingly lost art in our world, perhaps that means we are living among millions of narcissists. Narcissism is not a new phenomenon. The Internet and social media did not invent the condition, but they've certainly helped it to grow.

Normalizing Narcissism

You might be familiar with the legends of the ancient Greeks, such as Hercules or the Minotaur, and yet there is one story in particular that continues to strike a chord for me: Narcissus. The story goes that one day a young, handsome, and vain man named Narcissus goes out to the field to hunt. He eventually becomes quite thirsty and goes to the river to get a drink. As Narcissus leans down to the water to drink, he sees his reflection and falls in love with it, not knowing it is himself. When he bends down to kiss his reflection, it disappears, and he is left heartbroken. Despite the fact that he is becoming more and more dehydrated, he refuses to damage the reflection he loves.

Eventually Narcissus dies of thirst while staring longingly at his own reflection.

The conclusion? Perhaps the selfie isn't such a new thing.

Long before smartphones existed, Narcissus wasted away attempting to capture and stare at his beautiful face. As always, Greek mythology describes to us a long-standing, universal human truth: an infatuation with oneself. And with that we *have* created the normalization of the epidemic.

The culture we live in fosters and celebrates self-obsession with its excessive celebration of celebrity, fame, and wealth at any cost.

When it comes to studies of narcissism—and there are many—social media dominate the discussion. Science has linked narcissism with high levels of activity online with platforms like Facebook, Twitter, and Instagram.

A 2010 study from the University of Michigan found that the empathy of college students between 1979 and 2009 dropped off considerably after 2000, with the researchers speculating that the rising prominence of personal technology was one of the main factors.[*]

But wait! I promise it's not all doom and gloom.

Surprisingly (and pleasantly) enough, while walking the tightrope of social media and narcissism, the study hones

---

[*] Diane Swanbrow, "Empathy: College Students Don't Have as Much as They Used To," *Michigan News*, May 27, 2010, http://ns.umich.edu/new/releases/7724 -empathy-college-students-don-t-have-as-much-as-they-used-to, and Teddy Wayne, "Found on Facebook: Empathy," *New York Times*, October 9, 2015, http://www .nytimes.com/2015/10/11/fashion/found-on-facebook-empathy.html.

in on the positive outcomes of social media. The good news is that in the age of information, we can be more aware of what's going on in the world. We can see the entire world from our couch. Thousands of stories are at our fingertips. We have the ability to know about others around the world and, most important, who needs help.

Social media can actually facilitate social connection, and it might even *encourage* empathy. That study proved that "virtual empathy was positively correlated with real-world empathy."

Furthermore, a 2015 Pew Research Center report found that women with an average-size network are aware of 13 percent more stressful events in the lives of their friends than those without an account; for men, it was an 8 percent increase.[*]

Millennials, you're off the hook!

And there's more. While empathy, as studies suggest, can indeed be shared and felt virtually, in-person empathy—a hug as opposed to a "like"—has six times the impact of making someone feel emotionally supported.

That's the key. Nothing can replace real human contact. True human connection. That's why the key to normalizing narcissism is using social media in order to be more self-aware, *not* self-obsessed.

---

[*] Keith Hampton, Lee Rainie, Weixlu Lu, Inyoung Shin, and Kristen Purcell, "Social Media and the Cost of Caring" (Pew Research Center, January 15, 2015), http://www.pewinternet.org/2015/01/15/social-media-and-stress/.

I saw the world open up in my newsfeed this week: a friend gave birth to twins, a former roommate raised funds to donate goods to impoverished communities, a secretary at my old alma mater started chemotherapy for breast cancer and her Facebook group provided the community she needed in her last moments. I liked, commented, donated, and prayed over those updates. I saw the circle of life glowing through my LED screen.

Is all that really making a difference? Yes. It all has to do with intention. We can complain about generational differences and technological advances all we want, but at the end of the day, the world is only as compassionate as you yourself make it.

Maybe empathy can spread by being purposeful about when and how we use our little handheld world and find just one person who needs help. Maybe it's the new mom of twins, or the person organizing donations for a nonprofit, and maybe sometimes instead of *just* a "like," you ask the person to meet for coffee, give him a hug, and make six times the positive impact. But it starts with making yourself aware—and, sure, sometimes technology helps. And that's not always a bad thing either.

Mirror, Mirror

If Narcissus teaches us one thing, it's that we like to look at our reflection. Myself included.

In James 1, the author talks about looking at yourself in a mirror:

But be doers of the word, and not hearers only, deceiving yourselves. For if anyone is a hearer of the word and not a doer, he is like a man who looks intently at his natural face in a mirror. For he looks at himself and goes away and at once forgets what he was like. But the one who looks into the perfect law, the law of liberty, and perseveres, being no hearer who forgets but a doer who acts, he will be blessed in his doing. (James 1:22–25 ESV)

James uses the image of looking into a mirror as an analogy for one who hears but does not do what the Word says. I guess the best explanation for James's choosing the imagery of a reflection in a mirror is the fact that the average first-century reader had likely seen his or her reflection only a few times in his or her lifetime since mirrors were rare at the time. The early Christians were likely not as acquainted with their appearance as we are today.

Today, we can't imagine forgetting what we look like. We see our reflection and images daily, if not hourly. So how can James speak to us today when we have mirrors in every room and a camera full of selfies?

I think James knew something about the human condition: when we let the world dictate to us, we forget who we really are.

Instead of focusing on our reflection for purposes of

self-obsession (like Narcissus did), we should focus on hearing and doing practical and effective self-awareness, as James wrote:

> *Religion that is pure and undefiled before God the Father is this: to visit orphans and widows in their affliction, and to keep oneself unstained from the world.* (James 1:27 ESV)

So, what's the point of a reflection anyway?

It is to become self-aware. Or for the many other times it has made me aware of the leftover lunch in my teeth or unwanted, random chin hairs, the point of a reflection in the mirror is to make us aware of something we might not have seen otherwise. The point is not to obsess over it or forget about it. It's the linchpin for change. Only when I have become aware of my selfish heart can I begin to live differently.

That means we have an assignment! Much like the answer to fighting a self-obsessed digital world is to practice the compassion you wish to see, the answer to combating narcissism in our flesh-and-blood world is to practice empathy all day, every day.

Maybe we put down our phones an hour a day. Imagine the brain space we could free up and the opportunities we could make ourselves available to.

Maybe we *pick up* our phones, scroll past all the selfies and vapid noise, and find one person who could use something more than just a "like." You give that person a hug and make 600 percent more impact.

Or perhaps we volunteer somewhere once a week. There are organizations in nearly every community that work with the homeless, abuse victims, children in after-school programs, and refugees.

Does a single mom or a person with disabilities live in your neighborhood? Imagine if you offered to take their trash can out each week on collection day, a seemingly small act on your part that would bless them in tremendous ways.

Maybe it's carving time out of your week to lead a small group or Bible study in your home. This one is kind of selfish because leading a Bible study actually helps you as much as those you lead. (That's why teachers are brilliant in my mind: they're the ones who are always learning.)

Or what if you said *no* to the big opportunity to go out after work, which could potentially give you the influence and promotion you have been longing for, but went home and ate pizza and watched a movie with your family instead?

I get excited when I imagine a world where we learn to domesticate our savage hearts through the practice of empathy. It's through empathy that we can reach common ground with all humanity and be progressively liberated from ourselves. When we remember that God made us as well as every other living creature, we are dramatically reminded that we are not the center of this world or the next. Rather, we are a part of a big world, a world that is centered on God.

My little Andre Agassi is still pretty self-absorbed. In fact, as I'm writing this, he's staring at me and whining because he's ready for me to take him on his daily walk. I'm training him to be patient and realize we'll go when the time is right. What he doesn't realize is that I checked the weather report and I know the exact time the sun is going to break through those clouds and that pesky wind is going to die down, which will create perfect walking conditions. He's just got to trust me and wait, but it is hard to get this little narcissist to realize he doesn't know everything.

He'll get there.

So will we.

CHAPTER 3

Grief

When we honestly ask ourselves which person in our lives means the most to us, we often find that it is those who, instead of giving good advice, solutions, or cures, have chosen rather to share our pain and touch our wounds with a warm and tender hand. The friend who can be silent with us in a moment of despair or confusion, who can stay with us in an hour of grief and bereavement, who can tolerate not knowing, not curing, not healing and face with us the reality of our powerlessness, that is a friend who cares.

—HENRI J. M. NOUWEN

The first Sunday I braved going to church after Tennyson's death was awkward.

My parents are the pastors of the church I grew up in. When you're a pastor's kid, no matter how old, you're basically the mascot of the church. By this point, all of the church members had heard what had happened and were curious and full of questions. Many of them have known me since I was two years old when my parents started the church. I'm sort of everyone's "Little Tracy." They watched me grow and loved me through the years, and I know they really cared.

But I remember walking down the hall and seeing people who had been with me for every stage in my life look at me with the saddest eyes, then quickly look away. They didn't say anything. For a moment, I felt invisible.

I felt like I had leprosy.

My heart felt even lonelier, if that was even possible.

I discovered firsthand that many within the community of faith are uncomfortable with death and grief. Instead of reaching out with comfort and sincerity, there's an avoidance that actually adds to the pain and creates an awkwardness neither person knows what to do with. Death can complicate our theology about a good God, and it raises questions like, "Why do bad things happen to good people?" So we avoid any encounters by pretending the grief or griever is not there. We justify our avoidance by saying, "It's for the best that I don't say anything. After all, I'm likely to say something stupid." So instead, we say nothing and do nothing. We sit in silence with a mourner never acknowledging the loss or pain and pray he or she won't bring it up. All the while, the mother who lost her baby, the man who lost his wife of forty years, or the young woman who lost her soon-to-be husband all sit there wishing someone, anyone, would help them shoulder the overwhelming weight of their sorrow.

I didn't expect people to have answers for me. I knew

they couldn't answer why I had waited twenty-six years to fall in love and then lose him almost as quickly as he appeared. I knew they couldn't answer if I'd ever love or trust again. I didn't expect them to explain to me the theology behind theodicy and suffering. All I wanted, all I really needed (at least in the beginning), was empathy. I just wanted to feel, even if it was only for a moment, that I wasn't alone.

As the days and weeks went by, in my own effort to maneuver around the awkwardness, I often found myself comforting others who came up to me sheepishly and didn't know what to say. Trying to ease their discomfort, I convinced them I was fine.

So often it's easier to stay isolated and say, "That's okay. I'm fine," but in order to move past alienation and for empathy to flourish, the griever has to allow herself to be available to others. When grieving, a person's sensitivity is heightened. Everything—comments, looks, and remarks— is salt on a wound. My feelings got hurt over the smallest things that normally wouldn't have fazed me. If someone failed to invite me out for coffee, I thought my world was ending. Grieving can be ridiculously humiliating because of the emotional roller-coaster you ride every day. You're not sure if you are going to break down, stand still, or take a step forward. You're not sure how you are going to react to any given situation, so you avoid them. You aren't sure when a comment might make you want to fall apart. You are constantly feeling on the verge of an emotional breakdown, and it's embarrassing.

But I'm not ashamed of my grief anymore.

Perhaps, due to my faith tradition, I sometimes felt shame for grieving around "faith people." It was as if death and grief were a concession of my faith. *If I just had prayed more for my loved one, maybe he would not have died.* Often I felt I had to overproduce faith statements to appease those around me: "He's in a better place." "He's no longer in pain." "God is good." All these statements are true, but saying them wasn't helping me deal with the loss or the debilitating grief that felt like a cloud over my head everywhere I went. But if I said what I really felt, a blanket of shame would wash over me: *I'm afraid I'm never going to get over this. I can't sleep at night because I wake up with panic attacks. I need someone to sleep in the same room as me because I feel fear like a steady friend. I'm depressed. No one is ever going to love me again because I have so much baggage now. I'm so mad at God. I hate Tennyson. It's all my fault.*

How could I say those things?! That isn't faith. I should only be thinking, speaking, and believing positive things. I thought I was experiencing a theological dilemma, but I wasn't because faith is not the *absence* of reality. It's the belief that God is working in and in spite of those realities. But it took some time for me to realize that healing is a process that takes time, experience, and introspection.

If you've ever broken a bone, you know it's imperative to let that wound heal; otherwise, you might have even worse problems up ahead. The healing process might require rest, a cast, or maybe even surgery. Whatever the remedy your doctor recommends is the path you must take to heal the brokenness. The process is rarely convenient but always necessary. I've never broken a bone, but my heart was certainly broken, and the only way I was going to heal was to walk through the inconvenience of my grief.

Grieve with Grievers

I grew up in church, declaring the Word of God and believing that the Bible is living, active, and able to accomplish all that it was purposed to. I love the Bible and the workings of the Spirit because of my roots in faith. I also believe in the power of prayer and miracles. I believe God can and does heal today. But I also know that sickness does come and death sometimes follows. And when it does, God is still good; he still loves you, and is still in control of the whole universe. But I wonder if in the attempt to continually speak our faith into action, rather than accept any painful results, we lose the ability to know how to "weep with those who weep" (Romans 12:15). When someone has lost a loved one to cancer or to suicide, or has given birth to a stillborn baby, the rest of us have an opportunity to simply stop, look, and listen. It is our duty and calling to be a vessel of his love to those who are left to grieve.

In order to do this successfully, we need a theological starting point: Jesus. Okay, what does that actually mean? Well, for one it means when seeking an example of a life filled with empathy we need only to emulate or mirror his. So what does Jesus show us about empathy?

"Jesus wept" (John 11:35). If that's not empathy, I don't know what is.

Martha and Mary had lost their brother, Lazarus, and Jesus came to them to "wake him up." Upon Jesus' arrival,

> *Now when Mary came to where Jesus was and saw him, she fell at his feet, saying to him, "Lord, if you had been here, my brother would not have died." When Jesus saw her weeping, and the Jews who had come with her also weeping, he was deeply moved in his spirit and greatly troubled. And he said, "Where have you laid him?" They said to him, "Lord, come and see."* Jesus wept. (John 11:32–35 ESV, emphasis mine)

The Bible records in John 11:33 that Jesus was "greatly troubled." The Greek word, ἐνεβριμήσατο, which has been translated into our English word *troubled*, is maybe better understood as a display of indignation by Jesus. In other words, he was angry that something like death is a reality in this world. Not only does death upset Jesus; it enrages him because it's not what was ultimately intended. And despite the fact that he knew that he was about to raise Lazarus and restore joy to the family, he shows his humanity. Death appalls him too. He hates it. It is exhibit A of Satan's handiwork, and it made Jesus sick to his stomach. This should comfort those of us who have lost a loved one too soon. Jesus is just as troubled as we are.

However, this text has always perplexed me. Why would Jesus need to weep with Mary and the Jews with her? I realize he's showing his humanity in this moment, but that doesn't put his divinity on hold. He had to have known he was getting ready to raise Lazarus from the dead. So why the tears? Why not walk up to the grieving crowd and immediately announce the great miracle they are all about to witness?

John's gospel shows us a Jesus who stops to weep, grieve, and empathize with the brokenhearted first. It's true what the prophet Isaiah said: "A man of sorrows, and acquainted with grief" (Isaiah 53:3 ESV) was coming. In one of the most beautiful moments of the gospel, we see Jesus doing something many of us find weak, uncomfortable, and unnecessary. It's called empathy.

The Psalms of Silence

My quest to understand where spirituality, empathy, and grief intersect started with the Psalms. There's a reason that people gravitate toward these beautiful and poetic expressions in all seasons of life—from praise, to pain, to joy. The prose gives us words for when we are feeling thankful and it gives us the words we need to feel comforted and not feel so alone in our grieving. Even my most theologically minded, historically intelligent scholar friends have tattered Bibles with the pages from the Psalms being the most highlighted, ink-stained, folded, and worn.

But it's worth noting that the book of Psalms contains more lament than any other genre—more than thanksgiving and more than praise.

It was one such lament psalm that brought unbelievable and unexpected comfort to me. Psalm 13 is often referred to as the "how long" psalm and was written by King David:

> *How long, O LORD? Will you forget me forever?*
> *How long will you hide your face from me?*
> *How long must I take counsel in my soul and have*
> *sorrow in my heart all the day?*
> *How long shall my enemy be exalted over me?*
> (Psalm 13:1–2)

I love the person who is bold enough to ask a question that most of us are afraid to ask. In these verses, David is not afraid to ask God tough questions. They're tough because it is on saying and hearing his own words that the true depth of pain surfaces, and that can be overwhelming. While we don't know the reason for David's lament, we do know he's at the end of himself and has turned to God for help and comfort.

My dad taught me when I was young to read a psalm and a proverb every day, so I have likely read Psalm 13 hundreds of times. But it wasn't until I had experienced a life-altering moment that I could read it and understand the strange beauty in suffering and lamentation.

For years after Tennyson's death, I felt strangled by pain,

and often my best response to that pain was a desperate attempt at cheerful acceptance. Since God uses everything for our good and his glory, I felt that the most God-honoring attitude was to appear joyful all the time—even when I was angry, even when my heart was breaking.

I have since learned the beauty of lament. Lament highlights the gospel more than stoic acceptance ever could. Hearing our authentic, God-honoring lament can draw others to God in unexpected ways.

It certainly did for me. David's question to God, *How long?*, was now like reading my own words and heartfelt prayer to God. I too felt forgotten, abandoned, overwhelmed by my sorrow, and defeated. Before that time, I'm sure I read those verses and actually thought David was a bit irreverent and lacked faith. Now, his words feel real, authentic, and comforting. If David can ask God how long, then so can I. I've found that asking that question has drawn me closer to God.

During my grieving, I felt isolated in a cosmic sense—totally and utterly alone, and yet, during those long and sleepless nights, I often turned to the psalms—more often than not, Psalm 13. In those dark and lonely nights, my laments turned to prayers, which eventually turned to a song of hope.

I don't think it's an accident or coincidence that the psalms of lament outweigh the psalms of thanksgiving and praise. I think it's because the three are one in the same. Despite feelings of being forsaken by God, we all universally feel comforted when we're surrounded by people—his chosen people, to be specific—who understand life at its hardest. Lamentations mean that we understand inherently that God deeply cares for us through our tragedies.

And that brings me back to Lazarus.

The Greek word used to describe Jesus' weeping in John 11 is different from the word to describe the emotional state of Mary and the Jews. Their weeping is indicated as "loud wailing and cries of lament," whereas Jesus simply "shed tears," a beautiful and accurate picture of empathy.

You may find yourself in a moment of quiet grief with people who are feeling the deep pains of loss. During those times, empathy can look like someone who stops to listen to someone who is going through a divorce, or takes a walk alongside a friend who just lost a child, or gives money to a family that cannot buy groceries for the rest of the month—without expectation of reciprocity.

This kind of empathy isn't always convenient, comfortable, or easy, but it's a beautiful reflection of how we can live out kindness and compassion at home, at church, in our community.

In addition to the emotional side of grief, there is a practical side that shouldn't be ignored or overlooked. There are ways to address both aspects, whether for yourself or for someone you know. Here are a few things that helped me as I journeyed through my waves (and tsunami) of grief. It's certainly not a comprehensive list, but I hope it's a helpful starting point for you:

1. Read *Good Grief* by Granger Westberg. I give this tiny book to almost everyone I know who is working through sorrow. It's excellent for describing and explaining the stages of grief, which brings greater understanding of the whole process.

2. Get grief counseling. My grief counselor was the kindest and smartest older gentleman in the world. (He looked just like Santa Claus. I'm not totally convinced he's not Santa.) He listened to my cries, my fears, my guilt, and my pain-filled words. He was a safe place to talk and to listen. He painted an objective viewpoint and perspective of my grief that I could never have seen on my own. Sometimes I had no idea what we talked about each session, but I always left feeling a little lighter from the weight of my grief.

3. Cry when you need to (even if you're in the middle of Barnes & Noble). Give yourself permission to let the tears flow no matter where you are. But keep in mind that it's good to have an ample supply of tissues in many places: your car, every room in the house, your purse . . .

4. Journal. Write down everything you're thinking and feeling—just get it out. Emotions that are stuffed down and suppressed will eventually come out, and usually not in very pretty ways. Furthermore, one day you will go back and read those journal entries, and you'll be amazed at how far you've come.

5. Write a letter to the deceased. Whether it is a letter of love or confession or anything else—especially if there

was something between you left unresolved—write from your heart. For me, I had to write a letter to Tennyson forgiving him for what he had done . . . for leaving me the way he did. No one else in the world has ever seen or read that letter but me, yet it freed me from the anger that was controlling me.

6. Go to church, pray, and read your Bible. If you didn't go to church before this happened, consider starting. This may take some time, and that's okay. Just don't give up on God. He hasn't and won't give up on you. Sit in the back row if you want and let the rhythm and lyrics of the songs and hymns wash over your wounded heart and the Scriptures breathe new life again into your weary soul. Go to coffee with someone from your church, or attend a small group. Volunteer to be an usher or door greeter. Don't isolate yourself because that's when the enemy plays the most tricks with your mind. Stay connected to the community. Read David's laments in the book of Psalms or the red-letter words of Jesus in the New Testament. And pray, ever and always. God is listening to you.

My dad has had a lot of practice in comforting families in the wake of death in his more than forty years as a pastor. I once overheard him at a funeral tell a friend of ours who had just lost a family member, "I didn't know your loved one very well, but he's important to me because you are important to me." That's comfort! That's what empathy sounds like. I don't think we really understand how much it means to people when we're there for them in the big moments of their life. And not just for the funeral. Empathy is committing to being there for one another long after the flowers and cards stop coming. The sadness from grief really starts to set in after a loved one is buried or has walked out. Walking with someone through the journey is a healing balm that compares to none. The sacrifice of time and attention you make won't last forever, but the recipient will never forget the kindness and love shown at a time when others wanted to move on.

That first Sunday back in church was hard for me.

Really hard.

Maybe all I needed that day was for someone to come alongside, enter my world, and, just like Jesus, get troubled with my trouble.

CHAPTER 4

The Theology of Empathy

Imagination is not only the uniquely human capacity to envision that which is not—and therefore the fount of all invention and innovation—in its arguably most transformative and revelatory capacity it is the power that enables us to empathize with humans whose experiences we have never shared.

—J. K. ROWLING

Have you ever been on a blind date? I have. I've noticed that over time, many of my friends have taken it upon themselves to be my personal matchmaker (even though I have never asked them to be). A few years ago, a couple of friends thought I was just "perfect" for their single friend (if the word *perfect* comes up in the conversation, run away). They showed me a picture of him—a very nice-looking guy—and they begged me to let them give the nice-looking stranger my phone number. I obliged. A few days later, I received a phone call from him. He had a kind and strong voice and was easy to talk to. The conversation flowed, and he was easy to listen to. He asked if I would like to join him for a hike that weekend, and I agreed. As I hung up, I was excited about the potential. Who knows? Maybe this is "the guy."

Disclaimer: I don't think I'm too picky when it comes to dating (that's what every picky person says, though), but there are a couple of nonnegotiables for me. I'm just under 5'9", and with heels, I'm easily over six feet tall. So height is a big deal to me. It might not be for other couples, but I need a guy who is over six feet so that I don't feel like an Amazon woman towering over him when I'm wearing my favorite shoes.

When I got out of my car to meet the nice-looking stranger for our hike, I instantly knew this was not going to work: he was barely taller than I am. I tried to get the image of me towering over him in heels out of my head and tried to pay attention to what he was talking about, but there was no hope. As we hiked, it became even clearer that we were two very different people who were not "perfect" for each other as my friends had so believed. Our religious beliefs, politics, passions, fashion sense, and general taste in music were so different that I could hardly wait for the hike to be over.

The thing about relationships is that they are three-dimensional. I was ready to date the nice-looking stranger based on one photo and his kind, strong voice, but there was more to him. Once we met in person and although he was a wonderful guy, there just was no connection.

I think it's that way with God. We may know about God

from attending Sunday school as a kid or from what we have heard about him. But the moment you truly *know* God on a personal level, he exceeds every single one of your wildest expectations. He doesn't come up short, no pun intended.

God is present in our world.

God is present in our lives.

God is three-dimensional (and so much more) in our lives.

He is involved. He is intentional. He is intimate with us.

You've Got to Get Involved

Have you ever noticed that after getting a new car (or used, but new to you), you begin noticing "your" car everywhere? Before you had your new car, you don't remember seeing it. But now it feels as though the same make and model owns the roads you drive. It almost feels as if you're in a club with the other same-car owners.

In college, I drove a black Volkswagen Beetle. I remember noticing ALL the other VW Bugs driving on the road after I became a proud owner myself. I'm not sure if other automobile makes and models do this, but VW Bug owners honk and wave at one another. The first time I was greeted by a fellow Bug, I immediately felt a sense of belonging to a club I never knew existed. From that time on, I always made sure to pass along my greetings to fellow Beetle drivers down the highways. It didn't matter what color or year the model was, we were all part of the Beetle family. I had never realized just how many VW Beetles there were until I had mine. Isn't it funny how we can become aware of something that has always been there but we simply haven't noticed or realized it before?

Music has the power to make us aware of emotions and feelings we didn't know existed until our life takes us down a path that a lyric expresses in song. I could listen to the same song a hundred times but never really hear the words until something—good or bad—happens in my life that makes those lyrics come alive. It's as if that song all of a sudden speaks the language of my soul. For instance, I never understood the allure and total fandom of Taylor Swift's music until I had experienced betrayal, and then boom: it was as if T. Swift knew me and wrote her songs just for me. This is the power that can come from pain—a mutual connection and understanding.

After Tennyson died, I could quickly tell who else had suffered loss in their life as well. They were like the VW Bug club but for loss, and they all showed empathy toward me. Those other members knew there were no words that could eliminate the sting of betrayal or the right ointment to heal a shattered heart, but they understood that just showing up was sometimes all I needed. These club members, however, knew the words that would convey connectedness and give a sense of belonging and community in the center of deep loneliness. They would look me directly in the eye and say things like, "I'm so deeply sorry," "I love you,"

"I'm here for you," "Please let me know what I can do to help." They knew their words could never be the power or cure to the pain and sorrow I felt, but they were the comfort every hurting human longs for. Their actions and words said, *I care. You're not alone in this. You and your pain are not invisible. I may not understand exactly how you feel, but I empathize with your pain.* There's something about shared experiences. When someone has walked a challenging road similar to yours and has made it through the fog of pain, it makes you believe you will too.

This kind of shared experience and mutual understanding is the side of empathy that tends to be easier for all of us. However, there is another side of empathy, and it's not as easy for most people. That other side is when there's no shared experience or mutual understanding of someone's loss or circumstance. What do you do when you simply can't relate to someone's need or pain? Well, if you follow current trends, you're likely to do nothing. The modern dilemma when it pertains to empathy is that we avoid it, walk past it, ignore it, and let someone else do the job. But Jesus and the Bible offer us a much different portrait for the art of empathy.

If anything was embedded in my brain from the seminary, it was that we should not generally believe that experience alone should drive our theology. But if that's the case, why do we allow personal experience to drive what we do? The great myth is that empathy for others can come only through shared experiences. Hence, we generally empathize only when we understand or have gone through what someone else has gone through. I hear people all the time say you can't really empathize until you go through tragedy yourself. I don't believe this. I don't think this is what the Bible says either. It certainly isn't the example Jesus lived. Yes, empathy comes more naturally when you have a shared experience. Without a doubt, I have strong empathetic feelings toward people in my world who experience a sudden and tragic loss. I know those feelings—those haunting and terrifying fears. I know that sorrow. But if we all just sat around waiting for tragedy to strike before we started walking in compassion for one another, we would fall behind the curve and miss the whole point of what it means to be a part of the Christian story of extending care and compassion to others.

The Christian story is getting *in* the pit with your friend and riding out the struggle. Remember: em + pathy = *in* feeling. That does not mean writing cheerful scriptures or nice Christian clichés and dropping them in the pit where your friend is all alone. Empathy is getting in the pit with that person. There are a lot of pits I can't relate to since I haven't experienced them, so it's not as natural for me to just jump in. I'm not married, so my sweet friend whose husband walked out on her and is now dealing with custody and child support is a pit I jump into without much experience, but I'm there. I let her talk to me and cry and sometimes use choice words when discussing her ex. And sometimes we just shop, or go on walks, or have lunch and laugh our heads off.

I'm in the pit with her. Whatever she needs. On the tough days. On the good days. I'm not going to let her sit in that pit alone. One day she won't be in that pit anymore. Her life will eventually have a new reality. Life may never be what it used to be, but she's going to get through the struggle, the pain, and the betrayal that's there now. She's going to climb out of that pit and I'm going to climb out with her. But as long as she needs to cry, I'm going to cry with her. As long as she needs someone to listen to her, I'm going to listen. That's empathy.

I also do not have children yet, so for my friends who lost their baby just moments after he came into this world or to that couple who has been trying to conceive for years only to have a miscarriage—I will learn how to be there for them. I don't know what it's like to have dreams for your child and then see those dreams stolen by death. I cannot fathom the grief and overwhelming pain. But I'm going to climb down into that pit with them and be there not just in words but with actions.

All of us face sorrow, grief, conflict, and disappointments. The difference for Christians is that we don't journey through it alone. We have an indescribable comfort from an all-loving, good, and kind God. And one of our great missions on earth is to come alongside one another in his spirit of love as each of us navigates the painful and joyful roads alike. This is the great call for every Jesus follower. We've got to let our Christian mind-set drive our human actions.

• • •

At first when other VW Bug drivers honked and waved at me, I thought it was silly and basically a waste of time. But as the frequency of it increased over time, I decided if you can't beat 'em, join 'em. So I did. Not long after, I became the one honking and waving at every Bug in town. Then I noticed it's not just Bugs that have an exclusive club. The other day I saw two Corvettes driving down the highway, and as they passed one another, each driver gave a honk and a wave. I want to be in the Corvette club. Anyone else?

You've Got to Be Intentional

LA Consistency.

When people think of Los Angeles, they inevitably think of palm trees, the beach, terrible traffic, Hollywood, movie stars, and really, really ridiculously good-looking people (insert Zoolander voice). When I moved to Los Angeles to help pastor a Bible study in Hollywood, I quickly learned all these things are very true of LA—especially the terrible traffic part. I may or may not have lost my salvation a couple of dozen times driving two hours to move only ten miles. In almost any other part of the United States, you can drive ten miles in ten minutes.

This very true stereotype of LA is depicted in the *Saturday Night Live* spoof "The Californians." The cast of SNL parodies the LA obsession with beating traffic. Fred Armisen's character, Stuart, has some choice words for his antagonist, Devin (played by Bill Hader): "I think you should go home now, Devin! Get back on San Vicente. Take it to the 10, switch over to 405 North, and let it dump you onto Mulholland—where you belong!" If you have ever lived in LA, you get this.

I annoyingly found myself saying something similar whenever giving someone directions: "Just take the 10 to the 110 to the 101." One thing is certain about Los Angeles living: if someone is willing to drive you to the LAX airport rather than suggest you take an Uber, that is a real friend to hold on to.

The other thing I noticed about Los Angeles when I first moved there was people's inability to commit to plans. I noticed people would say, "Let's get together soon," but making an actual plan rarely followed. It usually was followed by a "I'll call you" or "We'll talk soon." Then at 4:05 on a Friday afternoon, you get a text from someone saying, "What are you up to tonight?"

I sat down to coffee with one of the women from the Bible study group that I was helping to lead when a light bulb went off for me. She told me how tough it is to connect with people in LA when it seems that most people don't want to commit to a plan. She explained to me the culture of not planning too far ahead *in case something better comes along*. Then, with tears in her eyes, she thanked me for agreeing to go for coffee with her last week and then not canceling on her.

It was sort of a "challenge accepted" moment for me. As a pastor, I knew I couldn't do everything for everyone, but I would at least start with being a consistent person in their lives. If I said I was going to be there, I would be there.

So I did the impossible in LA: I would make plans on Monday for something that wouldn't happen until Friday. When I began to do this, the person I was making plans with often seemed shocked. In fact, he or she would even suggest we see how the week goes and then we could confirm. But I would respond with, "That's okay. I'll be there Friday." And I was there Friday. I didn't call and change the plan after I received better invitations on a coveted night of the week. I showed up. I was consistent. Over time, I noticed people began to trust me to speak into their lives because I'd been showing up for quite a while. And to be honest, I didn't always want to. There were a lot of Friday nights that a "something better opportunity" came along and I wanted to cancel. But I knew that the only way I was going to have a voice in someone's life was if I lived consistently and intentionally.

I think this is one of the greatest ways we can live out the theology of empathy in our lives: by being intentional and doing what we say we're going to do. Make a plan and stick with it. Let your word truly be your bond. In a world where inconsistency rules, living a consistent and intentional life speaks volumes. I may have missed out on a few fun Friday nights by being intentional, but I'm sure I wouldn't have some of the great relationships in my life that

I do now. Consistency is an especially important ingredient for showing empathy.

You've Got to Be Intimate

Isn't it crazy how life is? When one person is rejoicing, another person is weeping? Even if your life seems to be halted, others' lives forge ahead. This was the shocking reality I had after Tennyson died. While Tennyson and I were dating, one of my good friends was also dating. But when my relationship ended in sadness, hers turned to pure joy when she and her boyfriend became engaged. She asked me to be one of her bridesmaids, which I happily accepted (P.S. I've been a bridesmaid fourteen times . . . I deserve a medal or something.)

I didn't want to be the Debbie Downer at her wedding, which took place just a few months after I had lost Tennyson and my own plans for a wedding were shattered. So I soldiered on and made sure the day was about her and her happiness rather than about me and my sadness. The wedding was beautiful and a memorable day for everyone. I was honored to be a part of it.

Years later, this same friend called me while going through an extremely painful and challenging situation in her marriage. The next evening, I drove to her house with dinner and ice cream in hand and stayed with her so she wouldn't feel alone in the midst of heartache. We sat and talked for hours. I listened and learned. We laughed and cried. I shared whatever lessons I had learned in my journey but never tried to compare our stories. I tried to point both our eyes to Jesus and all the wonderful things he is capable of doing in her situation.

At the end of the evening, with tears welling up in her eyes, she looked at me and said, "I'm sorry I wasn't the friend you needed me to be when Tennyson died. I was so wrapped up in my own world of getting engaged and planning a wedding while you were grieving. I wasn't the friend you needed, and now here you are sitting here being the friend I need and I don't deserve it." Now we were both crying. It was a healing moment for both of us and a moment that will be etched in my mind forever. Although my dear friend didn't feel she deserved the intimate empathy that I was extending to her, that's just what empathy is—it's intimate and devoted.

Empathy is getting your hands dirty and taking risks. You can do this only by being familiar and close to someone. This requires a lot of vulnerability on both sides. I had to let go of the expectations I had for how a friend should help me in my time of need and simply be the friend she needed at that moment. Easily and justifiably I could have been too busy or not interested in being there for her since she hadn't done that for me.

But just because she wasn't there in the way I wanted her to be years earlier didn't mean I shouldn't be there for her today. Maybe I wouldn't even know how to be the friend she needed today if I hadn't learned what it felt like to be alone in my dark days of grief and pain. I know what feeling alone feels like, and it's something I don't want anyone to experience. Walking in empathy means being an intimate friend, even if that person hasn't been that type of friend to you.

What Do You Believe?

For nearly ten years, my brother, Krist, and my sister-in-law, Kelly, tried to get pregnant. They saw doctors and specialists and took every vitamin and supplement imaginable and always believed one day they would conceive a baby. According to the doctors, it was never impossible for them to get pregnant, just tricky. But as months and years went by, there was still no baby.

All along God had been impregnating (no pun intended) in both Krist and Kelly the desire to adopt. As the years went on, the more they discussed the possibility and the more their hearts longed for it. No sooner had they decided this than they had babies, yes babies (plural).

In their adoption profile (which is what potential birth parents look at to make their choice of adoptive parents), Krist and Kelly had said they would be happy to adopt twins. Out of the blue on a Good Friday afternoon, they received a call from their social worker: "Come to the hospital and meet your sons." They hadn't known that a woman who had given birth to twin boys that morning had chosen them to be the parents to adopt the babies. That Easter Sunday I snuck into the hospital (against the social worker's orders) to meet my nephews, Westley Kenneth Wilde and Quincey Wendell Wilde. I absolutely fell in love.

A few months later, Kelly received a call from the twins' birth mother. Krist and Kelly had had an open adoption and a wonderful relationship with the twins' beautiful, selfless birth mom.

Side note: Women who give up their baby or babies for adoption are the most selfless and incredible women in the world. They are my heroes. I can't imagine being pregnant for nine months, going through the pain of labor, and then handing over my child to someone else. So in case you are ready to pass judgment on any birth mom, know that I will unleash a steady stream of contradictory statements that I would hope would change your mind on the subject. Soap box over.

The birth mom gingerly told my sister-in-law that she was pregnant again, and it was the twins' full sister. During the call, she told Kelly she couldn't imagine this little girl living without her two brothers but understood if it was too much to ask of them to adopt Westley and Quincey's little sister too. There was no question in Krist and Kelly's hearts or minds: that little girl was meant to be their daughter. So, thirteen months after the boys were born, little Whitney Opal Wilde (our WOW baby) burst onto the scene and right into our hearts.

When the boys were five and Whitney was four, something unexpected happened. Something we all probably didn't imagine would ever happen: Kelly found out she was pregnant. In the nearly ten years of trying, she never once had a positive pregnancy test. Not once. She probably took dozens upon dozens of tests, and this one time it said what she had longed to believe for years: she was pregnant.

Westley, Quincey, and Whitney were excited about their new baby brother or sister (in fact they hoped for one of each) and so was our entire family. We had been on this journey with them and couldn't wait to have a new little baby in our family.

After Krist and Kelly told the family the great news, they asked us not to share it with anyone else—yet I remember going away for the weekend after the big news and returned home to find that the entire world knew about the pregnancy. I teased Kelly for asking us not to tell anyone, yet she couldn't keep it in and was sharing the joyful news with everyone. Could you blame her? She had waited a long time for this moment.

A few months later, Kelly had a miscarriage. When she began spotting and experiencing pain, we all stood in faith and proclaimed life over that precious gift, but sadly our hope to meet that sweet baby on this side of eternity was not met. Our introduction would have to wait.

I didn't know what to say to Krist and Kelly. I didn't know how to help.

And I found myself thinking things like: *They shouldn't*

*have told anyone until the third trimester like everyone says.
At least they have Westley, Quincey, and Whitney. They'll get
pregnant again.*

I was embarrassed by my own thoughts. How inconsiderate and unempathetic could I be? They probably had similar thoughts themselves, but that's not what they needed from me. They needed me to get in the pit with them and just be there. They needed me to cry with them, to listen, to care.

So that's what I did. Did I know what I was doing? Nope. I had never experienced this kind of pain before, so I relied on what I believed about God: that he is present and available, so I was going to be present and available too.

What I believe about God shapes how I live my life and how I treat those around me. If my theology is that God is good no matter what and he is always there for the brokenhearted, then I better live as such. I want to live as such.

How can we be agents of empathy to a world that's beaten down and broken? I believe it starts with what we believe about God. Everything flows out of that belief. What we believe about him is going to determine how we live our life, how we treat people, and the decisions we make.

Eugene Peterson describes our beliefs as the most basic yet deepest dynamic about us. He writes in *Where Your Treasure Is*:

> *One of the great lies of the age is that what I believe is nobody's business but my own, that what I do in the secrecy*

of my own heart is of no account to anyone else. But what I believe is everybody's business precisely because what goes on in my heart very soon shapes the way I act in society. . . . Our beliefs are not off-the-cuff answers we give to an opinion survey; our beliefs are the deepest things about us. Our beliefs shape our behavior; therefore our beliefs are the most practical thing about us.

Peterson recalls the views of the great thinker and writer G. K. Chesterton on the topic of what we believe:

G. K. Chesterton once said that if he were a landlord what he would most want to know about his tenants was not their employment, nor their income, but their beliefs, if there was any way he could truly find out. For it would be their beliefs that would determine their honesty, their relationships, and their stewardship of the property. An adequate income is no proof against dishonesty. A reputable job is no guarantee against profligacy.

What we believe determines how we live, love, and lead. This is why our theology (what we believe about God) is essential for right living.

When I feel my theology doesn't cause me to love people more, I stop and reevaluate it. If our theology begins with ourselves rather than with Jesus, we will love only when we feel like it, empathize when it's convenient, and forgive those who deserve it. The problem with this formula is that love is not a feeling, empathy is antithetical to convenience, and the beauty and mystery of forgiveness is that no one deserves it (not even you). A good theology of a good God should always lead us to love and care for others more.

God is involved, intentional, and intimate in our everyday and ordinary lives as well as our tragedies and triumphs. God is very near and present in our lives. He is not far off and has not abandoned us, leaving us to fend for ourselves.

He's not only with us.

He's for us.

He's *in* us.

He's in feeling.

He's in love.

And that is why I will get in the pit with the hurting and broken.

God is there. And so am I.

CHAPTER 5

Who Is My Neighbor?

Do not waste time bothering whether you "love" your
neighbor; act as if you did. As soon as we do this, we find one
of the great secrets. When you are behaving as if you loved
someone, you will presently come to love him.

—C. S. Lewis

If you decide to write a book, expect to be challenged to live out what you are writing. The other day I was taking a writing break from this book so I could run to the store and grab some groceries for dinner. As I walked to my car with a full cart, I saw a man standing under a tree near my car, and he made full eye contact. At the same time, I noticed his wife approach me from the other side of my car. I thought they looked out of place in that Idaho is not exactly known for being culturally diverse. However, Idaho has welcomed hundreds of refugees. In fact, Boise, Idaho, has more Syrian refugees than both Los Angeles and NYC. By the way the couple in the parking lot were dressed I assumed they were perhaps refugees from that part of the world.

In my narrow-mindedness and my desire to load my groceries and get home, I immediately saw them as people who were about to get in my way. I started thinking things like, *Oh great. What do these people want? Here's a guy pimping out his wife to come ask me for something.*

I tried not to make eye contact with the woman as she walked closer and closer to me. But the next thing I knew, she was standing right next to me, about as close as another person can get without standing on top of me. She stood silently as I loaded my groceries into the trunk of my car. The man watched at a distance, also in silence. Since they weren't talking, I certainly wasn't going to talk.

As I pushed my shopping cart back to the cart corral, I heard a little whisper in my heart, *"Empathy."* Crap! You can't write a book about empathy and how we should love our neighbor and not actually do that. So as I turned around to walk back to my car, I intentionally made eye contact and smiled at the woman, who was still standing next to my car. As I got close, she uttered in broken English, "We have trouble." I looked deep into her eyes and asked what the trouble was. She answered, "Trouble with food." I didn't need a translator or to be a rocket scientist to understand they needed something to eat.

That little whisper in my heart struck again as I heard, *Who is my neighbor?* The answer was that at that moment, she was. That man was. They were. So I opened my wallet and gave her the little cash that I had, and with a big and genuine smile I handed her the money and said, "God bless you."

Honestly, I felt a little weird saying it. Couldn't I have thought of something more eloquent to say? I am a pastor, for goodness sake. You would think I would be better at these things. I don't remember the woman thanking me, but as I looked up, I saw the man still waiting by the tree, and with his hands clasped together, he nodded toward me in thanks. I thought about that man and woman the entire drive home. I wondered if I should have done more. *Wished* I had done more. Wished I would have been more like Jesus.

Months later I helped my church with a Thanksgiving feast for refugees in our city. I met families from Syria, Iraq, Pakistan, and the Congo. Through translators, each family told their story of coming to America and the fear of whether they would be welcomed or not. Many of them were fleeing war-torn countries that had devastated their homes and families. One man, who had been here for four weeks, explained that he was told that Americans would be mean and unwelcoming to him and his family. Thus the man came to the United States with a lot of fear for his family. But with tears in his eyes, he expressed to the room of strangers that he couldn't believe how welcomed he and his family felt. As I listened to each family share their stories I couldn't help but think back to the couple in the parking lot a few months earlier. Had they just arrived in their new country? Their new home? Was I one of the first people they encountered? Maybe I didn't do as much as I thought I should have—but hopefully I showed them a little bit of Jesus—the one who welcomes all of us and never walks past us.

The Fantastic Four

What I love about the Gospels so much is they are a beautiful history of the life of Jesus, and we are able to read them from four different perspectives. They were written by four different authors, each with a specific audience in mind. For centuries, people have tried to argue that the different perspectives nullify their accuracy. I couldn't disagree more. Each Gospel writer had a group of people and a certain message in mind as it pertained to him. Can you imagine if the Bible was inspired and written today only for Americans? Can you imagine if the Bible was written only for a blonde woman in Idaho? This would pose a great challenge for the rest of the world to comprehend the text as it related to them. The United States has language and cultural nuances that are distinct to us and not shared with the rest of the world. That's why the Gospels are written the way they are. They represent four lenses into the birth, life, and death of Jesus.* The Gospel of Matthew had the Jews in mind: Matthew quoted often from the Torah and referred to Jesus as "King" since he knew that's who the Jews were looking for. The Gospel of Mark was written primarily for the Roman Gentiles by the evangelist John Mark. Many scholars believe that for years Mark listened to Peter's firsthand accounts

---

* William Barclay, *A Beginner's Guide to the New Testament* (Louisville, KY: Westminster John Knox Press, 1995), Matthew: p. 2, Mark: pp. 6–7, Luke: pp. 10–11.

of being with Jesus. Hence, it is why Mark's Gospel is so power-packed from the outset. What evangelist doesn't love talking about signs and wonders? And the Romans of that day loved the power in his language. Luke's Gospel is the longest of the four (obviously; the smart ones have a lot to say). He writes with the Greeks in mind and focuses on showing readers the humanity of Jesus. The Gospel of John is written with the philosophical world in mind. John the beloved highlights the divinity of Jesus throughout his Gospel and gives us what I think are some of the most beautiful words in the entire Bible.

Because the four Gospels have four separate authors and different original audiences in many ways, they don't all share the same stories about Jesus and his life. I think this is a beautiful example of empathy. God provided multiple perspectives to speak to as many people as possible right where they are. For instance, Matthew and Luke share the beautiful nativity story of Jesus' birth, whereas neither Mark nor John mentions the birth. The compelling parable of the prodigal son is surprisingly found only in Luke's Gospel (Luke 14:11–32). The famous feeding of the five thousand is found in all four accounts (Matthew 14:12–21; Mark 6:30–44; Luke 9:10–17; John 6:1–15). All of the fantastic four (my name for the four Gospels) recount John's baptism (Matthew 3:1–17; Mark 1:1–11; Luke 3:1–22; John 1:15–34), and each gives considerable attention to the last week of Jesus' life, Holy Week.

The Gospels of Matthew, Mark, and Luke are referred to as the *synoptic Gospels*, which is translated as "seeing together." These three Gospels share many similarities, such as content and structure, as well as many events and sayings of Jesus. However, despite all the differences, all four Gospels have this in common: *Love your neighbor.* This is the Great Commandment. My favorite representation of this is in Luke's parable of the Good Samaritan.

If you grew up in church, you are likely familiar with the story of the Good Samaritan. But even if you were not, you still may know the famous anecdote of the only man who helped the beaten stranger on the side of the road. "Good Samaritan" has almost become synonymous with "good deeds." I venture to guess that if you did a Google search of "Good Samaritan" many nonprofit organizations that help those in need would pop up in your browser search.

Before we jump into Luke's version, I provide some historical background into how Matthew and Mark record the Great Commandment, which is taken from the Old Testament:

Matthew 22:34–40:

But when the Pharisees heard that he had silenced the Sadducees, they gathered together. And one of them, a lawyer, asked him a question to test him. "Teacher, which is the great commandment in the Law?" And he said to him, "You shall love the Lord your God with all your heart and with all your soul and with all your mind. This is the great and first commandment. And a second is like it: You shall love your neighbor as yourself. On these two commandments depend all the Law and the Prophets."

Mark 12:28–31:

And one of the scribes came up and heard them disputing with one another, and seeing that he answered them well, asked him, "Which commandment is the most important of all?" Jesus answered, "The most important is, 'Hear, O Israel: The Lord our God, the Lord is one. And you shall love the Lord your God with all your heart and with all your soul and with all your mind and with all your strength.' The second is this: 'You shall love your neighbor as yourself.' There is no other commandment greater than these."

The Pharisees loved the law. In Jesus' time, if you were a boy fortunate enough to attend school, you likely memorized the Torah (Genesis to Deuteronomy) by the age of twelve. It was ingrained in the minds of the Pharisees, so of course they despised Jesus for not adhering to the rituals and ceremonial laws embedded in the very fabric of their beliefs. The Sadducees were the upper-class sect of the Jewish community. These progressives of the day were highly influenced by the Greek philosophies of the first century. They rejected any notion of an afterlife and adopted an epicurean view of life on earth.

Thus, the thought of Jesus resurrecting and announcing a new heaven and a new earth was problematic for this group of socialites. The scribes of ancient Israel were also called teachers or lawyers (doctors of the law). They not only studied the law; they transcribed it. When there was a question of a legal matter, the scribes were consulted. These groups were constantly trying to catch Jesus saying and doing something contrary to the law. All these men would have read, studied, and even memorized the words Jesus recites—the words of their law in Leviticus and Deuteronomy.

With that brief background, we enter Luke 10 and the retelling of the Great Commandment in the parable of the Good Samaritan.

> And behold, a lawyer stood up to put him to the test, saying, "Teacher, what shall I do to inherit eternal life?" He said to him, "What is written in the Law? How do you read it?" And he answered, "You shall love the Lord your God with all your heart and with all your soul and with all your strength and with all your mind, and your neighbor as yourself." And he said to him, "You have answered correctly; do this, and you will live."
>
> But he, desiring to justify himself, said to Jesus, "And who is my neighbor?" Jesus replied, "A man was going down from Jerusalem to Jericho, and he fell among robbers, who stripped him and beat him and departed, leaving him half dead. Now by chance a priest was going down that road, and when he saw him he passed by on the other side. So likewise a Levite, when he came to the place and saw him, passed by on the other side. But a Samaritan, as he journeyed, came to where he was, and when he saw him, he had compassion. He went to him and bound up his wounds, pouring on oil and wine. Then he set him on his own animal and brought him to an inn and took care of him. And the next day he took out two denarii and gave them to the innkeeper, saying,

'Take care of him, and whatever more you spend, I will repay you when I come back.' Which of these three, do you think, proved to be a neighbor to the man who fell among the robbers?" He said, "The one who showed him mercy." And Jesus said to him, "You go, and do likewise." (Luke 10:25–37)

Similar to Matthew and Mark, one of the religious leaders of the day asks Jesus what is in the Law, and Jesus responds by reciting the Great Commandment. But the lawyer, we see in Luke, is only half satisfied with Jesus' answer and thus further probes, "Who is my neighbor?"

The lawyer, not unlike all of us, is actually asking, "Just how far reaching does my love and charity have to go?" In other words, "Whom exactly do I need to love to fulfill this requirement?" Can I give the woman in the parking lot all the money in my wallet and be good to go (thank goodness, it wasn't that much, right)? Through the parable of the Good Samaritan, we are invited into a definitive theological question: Who actually is my neighbor?

Jesus knew the lawyer wanted to trap him into making a heretical statement about obeying the law, so he flips the script and answers the question with a story, something at which he was masterful. He shares a parable about a Good Samaritan who was the only one to stop and help a man beaten and left for dead. There is a certain cadence to the story—Jesus tells it as if to make a dramatic point. He first tells us about a priest who sees the half-dead man and then passes by on the other side. Then a Levite sees the man and also passes by on the other side. Then enters the surprising protagonist of the parable, a Samaritan man. The Samaritan, just like the priest and Levite, sees the beaten and half-dead man but instead of passing by, he stops and has compassion. To give some perspective, Samaritans were racially mixed ancestors of Judaism and paganism. Around 700 BC the Assyrians conquered the northern land of Israel and captured their people. The captured Jews intermarried and adopted the pagan culture of the Assyrians even though they were half Jewish. The Jews of Jesus' day had a disdain for the Samaritans since they held an imperfect devotion to Judaism. Jews would refuse to be near a Samaritan so as not to be contaminated. With this cultural and historical context, can you imagine the Jews, with their centuries-long hatred for the Samaritans, listening to Jesus telling this story, which has a Samaritan as the *hero* of the narrative?

As Jesus closes his speech with this interesting plot twist, he asks the crowd which of the three men in the story is a neighbor. Of course, the lawyer and the crowd all recognized that the one who showed mercy was the neighbor— the Samaritan. It appears the question in Jesus' mind is not "Who is my neighbor?" but, "Am I a neighbor?" It feels as if Jesus is shifting the point of the narrative away from "who" is considered to be a neighbor to a question of whether we are willing to be a neighbor.

The real question becomes, am I a neighbor? This is the question I must ask myself. Am I willing to break the rhythm, routine, and customs of my day to see someone and have compassion as the Samaritan did? Or am I so busy with my own agenda that I see and walk past? This is the question Jesus was asking then and still asks us today.

When we read "love your neighbor as yourself" from ancient scripture, it is proper to interpret *neighbor* as all those in need.[*] If it's easier to understand, just replace the words *your neighbor* with *others*. To the Jews of the ancient world, their neighbors were Jewish neighbors. To Jesus, your neighbor was everyone—the whole world.[†] That's a lot of neighbors! But that isn't the whole point. The real question Jesus poses in Luke is not "who" is my neighbor but am "I" a neighbor. Am I the priest, the Levite, or the Samaritan in life? Do I stop when I see my "neighbor"/fellow human in need? I don't mean that every time you see a homeless person, you drain your bank account or invite a stranger to live in your home with your family (I thank God for the people who do, though). We all probably know people who interpret the text so literally that they live in a pathological state of serving everyone else that they forget to take care of their own health or family. Loving your neighbor as yourself does not mean we should stop loving and taking care of our own needs. That's illogical and unwise. But it does invite us into a new reality where we see others' needs as important, as well as the job of faith communities to care for one another.

---

[*] N. T. Wright, *Luke for Everyone* (Louisville, KY: Westminster John Knox Press, 2004), 127–28.

[†] Ibid.

Philosophy versus God

Recently a bunch of my family was together for a weekend at my parents' house, and we decided to go through some old pictures. My mom, aunt, cousins, siblings, and nieces and nephews started digging into the big box my mom brought out that was full of memories. Someone would show a photo and we would all laugh in unison over the memory or in shock over the awful photo we never wanted another human to see again.

The thing I learned from this walk down memory lane was that I apparently had no real friends when I was in my early twenties—because the things they let me do to my hair is what only an enemy would allow. Do you remember the show *Felicity*? Keri Russell's character, Felicity Porter, graduates from high school in Palo Alto, California, and is slated to attend Stanford, her father's alma mater, but instead chose a university in New York City because her longtime crush, Ben Covington (who barely knows she's alive), is going there.

The show follows Felicity and her friends throughout the highs and lows of their college lives. Felicity has naturally curly hair (really curly hair, like perm curly), and so do I. In the second season, Felicity decides to cut off her long curly hair into a short curly pixie cut as a sign of freedom or rite of passage or some other nonsense. But for some reason, I thought it was a great idea, and so I decided to copy that. Worst idea ever.

First, Felicity's haircut was such a bad idea that some say it nearly tanked the show. The ratings plummeted, and the show eventually moved to a different night and time, not a good sign for a television show. If adorable Keri Russell couldn't pull that hairstyle off, what on earth made me think I could? I tried to salvage my terrible decision by coloring my hair red. I do not have the proper coloring for red hair. Oh. My. Word. Where were my friends? I have basically tried to destroy every photo with evidence of this time in my life, which I refer to as "the lost years."

Thank goodness, hair grows and hair colorists could bring my hair back to blonde.

Much like my fleeting choices in hair, this once-red-head-rocking-a-pixie-cut was jamming out to every boy band known to humanity. I'm happy to report that I'm now a midlength blonde whose musical taste has matured. The same things could be said for our many and always-evolving philosophies. I of course hold my own philosophies about life, politics, fashion, and even hair and music, but I hold them loosely since they often change, because I change. Yes. Thank goodness, we change.

The word *philosophy* comes from the Greek *philosophia*—*philo* meaning love and *sophia* meaning knowledge or wisdom—and therefore meaning love of knowledge. So if philosophy is the love of knowledge, philosophies by definition grow, emerge, evolve, and change because we're learning new things.

When you elevate your evolving and often-misguided philosophies over the care of people, you've missed the point. Think about the parable of the Good Samaritan. It was the passionate philosophies of the priest and Levite that kept them from caring for the half-dead man on the side of the road. Remember that both the priest and Levite held tightly to the ancient Jewish tradition that those cursed or dead were unclean; anyone who touched them would also become unclean. To be fair, they were traveling from Jerusalem to Jericho, which indicates they were likely on their way to Jericho to participate in offering a sacrifice. For all intents and purposes, the man is described in the Bible as being "half-dead," which must have meant the Levite and the priest could not know for certain whether he was dead. If he was in fact dead and they touched him, they would be made ritually unclean according to the Torah (Leviticus 21:1–2) and unable to offer their sacrifice. This was a religious philosophy that ancient Jews held passionately and vehemently. They couldn't risk becoming unclean.

The priest and the Levite are caught in a moral dilemma. What would be better: to disobey the law and risk becoming unclean or disobey the law and not love your neighbor as yourself? They didn't want to risk compromising their philosophy or religion in order to care for a person. But the surprise of the narrative is the Samaritan—the one who was likely the religious enemy of every character in the story, who abandoned his personal and cultural philosophies to live like Jesus and to have compassion enough to put it into action. The biggest shock is that in spite of the deeply rooted hatred between Jews and Samaritans, the Samaritan overpowers his hatred with love.

When your philosophy becomes more important than a person, it has failed you. There is nothing more dehumanizing than to care more for a philosophy than a living, breathing person. People are the priority. People are God's priority. That being said, philosophies and God's Word are different. Think about it this way. Philosophy is what I think is the best hairstyle (right now). Not to dangerously over-simplify, but for the sake of metaphor God's Word is the natural makeup of your hair. Mine is curly and it will always be curly; the natural tendency of my hair is unchanging. That's just the truth. (Sorry to all my seminary professors if this is far too simplistic and a theological stretch.)

We often look at our personal philosophies about life, people, and the Bible as if they are deeply rooted and proven theology. They are not. They are closer to opinions. They are provisional. Philosophy is what we believe is true. God's Word is what we know to be true. One should be held loosely; the other should be held steadfast.

God's Word doesn't change, emerge, or fail. It is steadfast and eternal. This is why our personal philosophies should be shaped by our understanding of God rather than our under-standing of God being shaped by our personal philosophies.

Of course, philosophies are important to have; it's the de-velopment of philosophy that keeps us learning and growing. However, no matter how much we love them, they should never be held with greater importance than knowing God. An undeveloped philosophy on empathy could potentially keep us from living out the great story God has planned for us. Em-pathy challenges our tightly held beliefs and moves us to love those who might be our cultural and religious enemies. This takes courage—the same courage that caused the Samaritan man to stop, see, and have compassion on the half-dead man.

The Normal Neighbor

It should surprise no one to hear that Christians are supposed to have an impact on the world. Like the biblical followers of Jesus, followers today should be turning the world upside down with their outward expressions of faith. However, when we think about "biblical impact" and "turning the world upside down for Jesus," we often hear that we've got to live "radical" lives. That is, we need to sell our Volkswagen, give up all Hollywood movies, and relocate to the deserts of the Middle East in order to do some good.

And yes, that would be great if we all felt called to do that. The reality, however, is that the large majority of believers don't and won't quit their jobs, sell their stuff, and pack their bags to head out to "enemy" territory.

Why?

Fear.

Fear of the unknown. Fear of being in uncomfortable situations. Fear of possibly getting killed.

However, the truly unfortunate fact is that we don't have to think about living radical lives to experience this fear. We already struggle with it in our normal everyday lives.

The Western mind has grown accustomed to a steady diet of fear rhetoric. *Terrorism is real, so be careful of refugees. That candidate is going to destroy our country and cause a world catastrophe, so don't trust him. The economy could crash any second, so don't live with a generous open hand. If you love the sinner, you are sending a message that you con-*

done that person's lifestyle. What this means is that we go to the grocery store down the street and have totally unjustifiable thoughts about an innocent stranger.

Allowing fear to dominate our thinking and actions paralyzes us as Christians. It keeps us from living like Jesus in a world that so desperately needs him.

But I have good news: God is not intimidated by the threats of terrorism, threats to biblical living, or the decisions by world leaders. God tells us throughout the Bible *not* to fear. I have heard it said that there are 365 "fear nots" in the Bible, one for every day of the year. I think that is a pretty good case for us to believe God really doesn't want us to fear. Fear is the enemy's successful tool for holding us back and holding us hostage.

The Bible promises us that we don't have a spirit of fear; rather, we inhabit a "spirit of power, love, and a sound mind" according to 2 Timothy 1:7 (NKJV). That sounds a lot more like a sound theology of empathy to me.

God is calling Christians to simply care about what God cares about.

God calls us to be normal neighbors—and neighbors are meant to be (surprise!) neighborly.

An empathetic life looks like normal, everyday love for our neighbors. It's less about being "radical" (which, again, is 100 percent awesome) and more about showing grace and kindness in the small, daily moments.

Empathetic living doesn't always have to be astonishing. It might be hosting a brunch in your backyard, or putting together a neighborhood baseball game, or going grocery shopping for your neighbor, or showing up and participating in your annual HOA meeting (P.S. this is a great way to meet your neighbors). As we open our hearts and our doors, we practice empathy by caring for local children or bringing a homeless person home for dinner or even just having neighbors over for a movie night. Empathetic Christians befriend people and extend their reach to outsiders and strangers. They embrace those in physical and spiritual need (which I'm pretty sure is everybody).

The most interesting aspect about the Parable of the Good Samaritan is that we have no idea who the half-dead man is. We know from Scripture that he has been robbed and stripped of his clothing, leaving us no sign of either his nationality or social ranking (both of which were indicated by clothing in ancient times). He's an unidentifiable human. There's no way to know if he is rich or poor, powerful or powerless, or a friend or foe. This is an essential part of the story. It's one thing to be a neighbor to someone you think deserves your care and compassion, but it is an entirely different story when the person could very likely be your enemy. The Parable of the Good Samaritan does more than convince us to stop, see, and have compassion for others—it intends to smoke out our biases as to who we believe deserves our empathy. I certainly don't think that the money I gave to the woman at the grocery store was either courageous or enough. I could have done more. I probably should have done more. But what I did do was break a paradoxical claim and philosophy I tightly held about who is my neighbor. Empathy drove me to stop, see, and love someone whom I easily could have passed by.

CHAPTER 6

Compassion Fatigue

Never worry about numbers. Help one person at a time and always start with the person nearest you.

—Mother Teresa

When I was nineteen years old, I went to southern India on a church missions trip. I had been on other trips like this before but not to a Third World nation like India. We spent several weeks giving basic necessities (e.g., toothbrushes, toothpaste, brushes, deodorant) to orphans, widows, and those living with the effects of leprosy throughout southern India. I hadn't realized leprosy existed outside the New Testament until this trip. We went to leper colonies where we gave basic care packages to men, women, and children who were missing limbs, parts of their face, and disfiguring sores and lumps all over their bodies.

I was overwhelmed by the need I saw as we stood side by side and worshipped God with these beautiful people. They greeted our young American missions team with big smiles and hugs. They were so grateful not only for the necessities we brought them but the kindness and companionship that came with them.

As you know, India has a caste system. This social class structure places these poor victims of leprosy at the bottom of their caste system. Just as in the Bible, they are the lowest of the low. Christian mission in that part of the world has provided relief and comfort to these neglected people. One thing that astonished me was the joy that permeated those people. Each colony is located far from civilization, and inhabitants do not have much, if any, contact with the rest of their society. But they were all full of joy.

We also visited schools, orphanages, and widows' homes. The widows broke my heart as much as the leper colonies had. These women (ranging in age) are basically living in a sort of orphanage for women who have lost their husbands and have no social or economic standing in their country. I will never forget one beautiful widow who grabbed my face and, with tears pouring down her face, began praying for me. The translator who was traveling with our team quickly came over to translate her prayer. She was praying for America and me. She said if God would save America, then the whole world could be saved. Tears were now cascading down my face too, and I was overcome by this woman's boldness to pray for the United Sates and me. These widows pray hours upon hours a day for America. I felt so convicted for not having this same fervency for my own nation (or for theirs).

At the conclusion of our trip, we stopped in Mumbai, where I was introduced to the shocking reality of the sex trade industry. On one of our last nights there, our group was taken, with little information, to a building where we were escorted into a room. We met several young girls between ages ten and fourteen who had been sold by their parents for sex trafficking. They had just been rescued from that life. I was shocked, angry, disgusted, and confused. I had never heard of sex trafficking before. It wasn't on the news and very few people were yet involved in rescuing these children from the heinous and enormous reality.

If leper colonies, orphans, and widows weren't enough to set me in sensory overload and assault my emotions, then imagine meeting young girls who had been forced to service dozens of men a day. I couldn't get out of that country fast enough.

When I returned to the United States, I didn't talk about the trip to anyone. When people asked me how India was, I replied, "Fine," and walked away as quickly as I could. If I smelled curry, I would run the other way. Even when my family wanted to hear stories and know more about this once-in-a-lifetime trip, I said nothing. I had purchased all my friends and family gifts along the journey—some of the gifts were candles made by the kind men and women I met in the leper colony—but I shoved them into a closet for six months instead of giving them to the designated recipients simply because I did not want to talk about it or think about what I had seen. I was overwhelmed by the need, and my compassion shut down. I was compassion fatigued, a term coined by psychologists to describe those (particularly care-

givers, physicians, nurses, therapists, and emergency work-
ers) who work with trauma victims and gradually become
overwhelmed or burned out and lose compassion for those
in their care.

The term *compassion fatigue* has been around only since
the early 1990s and has also been referred to as "secondary
traumatic stress." It is often the process before total burn-
out, particularly in helping professionals and caregivers.
Charles Figley, one of the leading voices in education and
psychology, has written extensively on the topic of compassion fatigue—for example, "The professional work centered
on the relief of the emotional suffering of clients automatically includes absorbing information that is about suffering.
Often it includes absorbing that suffering as well."[*] It is this
absorption of someone else's suffering that can often lead to
a form of compassion fatigue if we're not careful.

In the Arms of an Angel

Four words: Sarah McLachlan dog commercials. Many of
us, even the animal lovers among us, immediately change
the channel as soon as we see Sarah and hear her song
"Angel" for the American Society for the Prevention of

---

[*] "Compassion Fatigue as Secondary Traumatic Stress Disorder: An Overview," in
*Compassion Fatigue: Coping with Secondary Traumatic Stress Disorder in Those Who
Treat the Traumatized*, ed. C. F. Figley, vol. 2 (New York: Brunner/Mazel, 1995).

Cruelty to Animals (ASPCA) commercials. I'm pretty sure these are the most depressing commercials on TV . . . ever! Even Sarah, in a recent interview,* admitted she changes the channel because "it just kills me." I'm not sure how much money or awareness ASPCA receives from these commercials, but I get it: from a marketing standpoint, these commercials are brilliant because they are widely known and talked about. But come on, it's too much . . . I just can't watch. The other day I heard the song on the radio and had to change the station because it conjured up images of sad puppies and I just don't need that.

Our endless access to media, which can be a deluge of images and stories of tragedy and suffering taking place all over the world, is a major culprit of compassion fatigue in the Western world. We have become overwhelmed by need. Consider the evidence.

Since the inception of the twenty-four-hour news cycle, we have been inundated with images of mass tragedy. In 2001, we saw live television of planes hitting the Twin Towers in New York City. CNN, Fox News, MSNBC, and every other news affiliate showed vivid video images of people jumping out of the towers to their inevitable death. We heard the sounds of a once magnificent building tumble to the ground in seconds and a pillar of smoke soar to the sky

---

* Danielle Anderson, "Sarah McLachlan Reveals How She *Really* Feels About Her 'Brutal' ASPCA Commercial," December 28, 2015, http://people.com/celebrity/sarah-mclachlan-aspca-commercial-singer-reveals-how-she-really-feels/.

in its place. We watched this and heard the screams. More than 3,000 people lost their lives that September day.

In 2004, we watched as parts of Indonesia, Sri Lanka, India, and Thailand were devastated by what is being called the worst tsunami in history: 230,000 people lost their lives. News pictures and videos showed corpses hanging from trees or washed to shore days later, where they almost immediately rotted in the tropical heat.

In 2005, Hurricane Katrina took the lives of over 1,800 Americans. Not long after that were mass shootings at Virginia Tech, Fort Hood, and Sandy Hook Elementary School. Completely innocent lives taken. And these are just a few of the examples of tragedies that have occurred over the course of the last fifteen years.

After a while, these catastrophic natural disasters and all-too-frequent mass shootings become too much to look at. We feel sad. We feel pain for those who lost loved ones, but we no longer empathize. We might post a beautiful tribute on social media such as adding the French flag filter over our Facebook profile picture or post an Instagram with the hashtag "Pray for Paris" following the 2015 Paris terrorist attack. But we've become so numb to tragedy that these tributes become our best attempt at empathy and resolve to appease a sense of moral obligation. If this compassion lethargy goes unchecked, it can lead us to a narrow view of how we should care for those we are the closest to.

●　　●　　●

We can't get away from tragedy. This past year alone was full of catastrophic heartbreak, with hardly a break in between each event. One week in 2016 in particular shocked us to our very core. On June 10, 2016, the up-and-coming pop star Christie Grimmie was fatally shot by a stranger before her concert in Orlando, Florida. Two days later, on June 12, not even before we had begun to grasp the scope of Christie's sudden death, there was a mass shooting in an Orlando nightclub, Pulse, with forty-nine people killed and fifty-three more wounded. This has been considered the deadliest terror attack on U.S. soil since September 11, 2001. Three days later, on June 15, we were horrified to learn that a two-year-old boy, who was wading in less than six inches of water at a Disney World resort, was snatched by an alligator who pulled the boy underwater where he drowned as his dad frantically tried to save him. This came off the heels of the world seeing the video of a gorilla at the Cincinnati Zoo dragging a three-year-old boy around the gorilla enclosure after the boy fell in. The boy was rescued unharmed, but the traumatic video footage was seen over and over around the world and was still fresh in our minds. And just when you felt ready to come up for air, another terrorist attack claimed eighty-six people's lives on June 15, Bastille Day, in Nice, France.

The worst for me has been the haunting image and video of a little boy caught in the middle of a Syrian airstrike on August 18. Omran Daqneesh, believed to be five years old, had been rescued from a building and brought to an ambulance where he sat traumatized, covered in blood and dust. He's the same age as my twin nephews, Westley and Quincey. He's just an innocent boy, caught in the middle of a tragic reality of hatred and war.

We don't know what to do with these images that assault our senses. We feel sad but know our sadness is not enough. We want to do something but don't know where to start. We feel numb and overwhelmed, so we shut down. We go on with our day getting our coffee from Starbucks (or whatever other coffee place you love) on our way to work, pick up dinner at Whole Foods on our way home, and sit in front of our TV. I feel so overwhelmed that I don't know where to begin, so I don't begin at all. The neuroscientist Sam Harris speaks to our ability or inability to respond to human suffering in his book *The Moral Landscape*. Harris cites the work of psychologist Paul Slovic on how we respond to the suffering of other people:

> *Slovic's experimental work suggests that we intuitively care most about a single, identifiable human life, less about two, and we grow more callous as the body count rises. Slovic believes that this "psychic numbing" explains the widely lamented fact that we are generally more distressed by the suffering of [a] single child (or even a single animal) than by a proper genocide. What Slovic has termed "genocide neglect"—our reliable failure to respond, both practically and emotionally, to the most horrific instances of unnecessary human suffering—represents one of the*

*more perplexing and consequential failures of our moral intuition.**

Harris diagnoses a grave reality that many of us can identify with. Unfortunately, his prescription (a proud atheist) leaves little hope.

Christians, among all civilization, should have the right prescription. As Christians, we have a sense and understanding of moral obligation. Yet even when we feel too much, we shut down (compassion fatigue), and if we shut down and don't feel anything, we don't act.

Compassion International

If you have attended a major church conference around the world lately, you have likely heard of Compassion International, one of the leading charities in the world. Compassion International offers the opportunity for you to sponsor a child from an impoverished part of the world where your donation will provide a child with food, education, and medical assistance. What I think Compassion International does so well is taking a massive need and bringing it down to a size and level that's feasible to participate in.

If someone were to tell me how many children are

---

* Sam Harris, *The Moral Landscape* (New York: Free Press, 2010), 69.

starving around the world, or orphaned, or in need of education or clothing, I would likely shut down. Not knowing what to do with such a huge problem becomes overwhelming to me. However, when you show me one child, the face of a five-year-old girl, and you tell me her name is Emili, she was born in Ecuador on August 2, 2013, and she likes to play with dolls when she's not responsible for performing chores for the family, that is something I can connect with. Something I can give to and see palpable results.

Sam Harris points out that this is the human condition: "When given a chance to donate money in support of needy children, subjects give most generously and feel the greatest empathy when told only about a single child's suffering. When presented with two needy cases, their compassion wanes."*

Compassion fatigue strikes when we recognize how great the need is and we know we can't physically or geographically fill that need. Although my heart ached when I saw the images of young Omran Daqneesh caught in the middle of a war that he neither started nor understands, I knew there was nothing I could do to help him besides pray. Prayer might seem little and insignificant, even a cliché, but it's not. In that moment, all I had was prayer. As

---

* Ibid.

I prayed for that boy and everyone else caught up in the Syrian conflict, God began to open my eyes to areas right here in my own world where I could live out the narrative of empathy.

I was reminded in that simple prayer how I could finally go out for coffee with that friend who has been asking for months. I also felt God encourage me to meet and get to know all my neighbors on my cul-de-sac. I've met nearly all of them but have a few more to go. I also felt prompted to give a gift card to Big Al's to the Syrian refugee family I met at our Thanksgiving outreach—I heard they wanted to try bowling and spend time as a family but didn't have the extra money for activities. Maybe I can't get to Syria and help, but I can certainly show love to the Syrians right here.

Thinking about your first job will give you some insight into empathy. We all know we don't start as the CEO. We usually are hired as an intern or for another entry-level position. Eventually, if we work hard, we are promoted and move up the ladder. Empathy works the same way. We don't have to start by running into combat rescuing children or freeing men and women from ISIS (although some of us can). It starts by my knowing my next-door neighbors' names. And if I see their car pulled over on the side of the road, I stop and help instead of zipping past. It starts as well with leading a small group of college students every week to teach them about God and the Bible, because what might happen is that one of the members devotes her life to a ministry in the Philippines to rescue children from the terrible reality of sex trafficking. I may never go to the Philippines or work for a ministry like Wipe Every Tear, but Ebie Hepworth, the young woman I led in that small group, did.

God is not intimidated by the world's powers. He truly is in charge of the whole cosmos. And he hasn't gone off and left the world to fend for itself, so there is no need to worry about that. But to think God is going to send us to Syria to rescue hurting people when we have neglected to rescue those hurting in our homes, neighborhoods, churches, and schools is to forget that God loves the whole world, even your tiny slice of it. Listening to understand my friend's point of view is a starting point. Meeting my neighbors and participating in community with them is a starting point. Helping international students and refugees feel welcome in your city is a starting point. It might seem small, but there's a great passage in the Bible about small things: "Do not despise these small beginnings, for the Lord rejoices to see the work begin" (Zechariah 4:10 NLT).

Imagine if we all started showing empathy in the small areas. Think how quickly and easily we could then tackle the big areas. I believe that when we obey God and do the "small" things, like loving our neighbor, it has a direct and divine impact on the big and sometimes overwhelming needs in the world. It's amazing how we can change the world by simply walking out our front door.

Practice Makes Pathos

Like so many moms do, mine had me take piano lessons as a kid. My parents were great at letting my two older siblings and me choose whatever sports we wanted to play, but piano was nonnegotiable. I come from a fairly musical family and have always loved music and singing. In fact, my mom said I sang before I talked. Every Monday morning, she said she would wake to hearing me hum the melodies of hymns sung the day before at church.

Because I've always loved music, my mom naturally thought I would thrive in learning piano. But thrive is not even close to my experience with the piano. I certainly loved and fantasized about the idea of playing the piano in front of an appreciative audience, but this fantasy never included practicing. There are only so many hours in a day, and I didn't want to waste them practicing for an hour in the living room. My memory is of a dark, cold, stale room that we used only during holidays or when special guests came to visit—and then I had to be on my very best behavior, so it was the boring room for me! I loathed my afternoon piano practice almost more than anything else in the world, so as you can imagine, I didn't advance very quickly.

Each week, my patient piano teacher graciously smiled when she asked if I had practiced this week, and I stuttered to get out something like, "A little bit, Mrs. Tarter." Each lesson I learned something new and promised myself that

I was really going to practice, but each week the cold, stale living room seemed unwelcoming.

A few years into my lessons, Mrs. Tarter noticed a spike in my piano ability around Christmastime. What she discovered was that I loved Christmas music and happily practiced for hours. So instead of giving me my Christmas piano lesson book in the fall (as she did with all the other students), she began giving me mine in July. My piano career never really took off, but I can play some good Christmas tunes.

Similar to what Mrs. Tarter discovered about me, we all must discover ourselves: we practice what we like or what we want to practice. And the human fallacy is that we struggle to practice what we don't like.

The problem with most people (including me) is we don't like to practice. I think we like the *idea* of something, but we don't want to put in the effort to attain it.

Colossians 3:12 tells us to "put on" compassionate hearts and kindness and wear them like they are clothes. Putting something on indicates to me that it's not inherently there. You weren't born into the world wearing clothes. You were born butt naked, and you certainly wouldn't leave your house without putting some clothes on now. Right?

You know who might leave the house without putting clothes on? Kids! They haven't yet developed the practice of getting dressed every day. In fact, my five-year-old nephew Quincey had to be convinced that he couldn't wear just his undies to kindergarten.

That is what Paul is trying to drive into the minds of

these neophyte Christians in Colossians. They have to practice every day "putting on" mercy, compassion, kindness, and love. It's not natural. We weren't born automatically kind, loving, and forgiving.

We like the *idea* of being kind and loving, but often we're content to study a concept more than we want to actually practice and apply it. This was true of me when I was deciding whether to go to law school after college. I received my bachelor's degree in political science, and the next logical step for poli sci majors typically was law school. In fact, some of my favorite courses as an undergraduate were Constitutional Law, Brown vs. Board of Education, and History of the Supreme Court. I seemed destined for the law.

When the political science department hosted a forum with a professor from Harvard Law School, he invited me to attend classes at Harvard and see what I thought. In fact, he said, part of his trip was to recruit women from western states to attend Harvard.

A few months later, my parents were heading to Rhode Island to speak at a church, and they invited me to tag along so we could drive together to Boston and visit Harvard Law School. I emailed the professor who had invited me, and his assistant promptly set up a tour and classes for me to attend. As I walked through the campus, I was awestruck. I sat in the back of a class imagining all the men and women of history whom I had studied about for years—Supreme Court Justice Oliver Wendell Holmes Jr. and President Rutherford

B. Hayes, for example—and wondered if they had once sat in this very classroom. (For all my fellow *Gilmore Girl* fans, it was a very Rory moment for me.)

After returning from Boston, I purchased several admission test prep books and began ferociously studying for my Law School Admission Test (LSAT). I had connected with another professor at Harvard who was on the admissions board and reiterated the desire to accept more female students from western states. I was motivated! I needed to do well on my LSAT and finish my bachelor's degree with strong grades. The only problem was that I really didn't enjoy the practice and timing section of the LSAT prep books.

I had learned from many other previous test takers, and from the LSAT review course that I attended, that the key to success on the LSAT is timing, so you have to practice getting through all the questions. I timed myself with a few of the practice exercises in the prep book and convinced myself I had practiced enough.

I just didn't like practicing.

I should have recognized the omen right then. One of my friends who had decided to drop out of law school told me she realized she liked *studying* law but really didn't want to *practice* it. As she said that, I realized I too had never considered the idea of practicing law. All I was focused on was studying it. Sure, I loved studying law, but the thought of being an attorney with mile-high paperwork and endless litigation made me feel sad inside.

If I needed any more proof that practice wasn't my forte, my LSAT score confirmed it.

I think this is similar to how Christians look at our role in the Christian narrative. We like to go to church on Sunday and hear an encouraging sermon or attend a Bible study or small group where we feel an intimate sense of community. However, when life forces us to practice the things on Monday that we heard and learned about on Sunday, we falter. The Christian way is merely a theory in our life until we begin to practice it, and through our actions, we prove its validity to the world. Otherwise, how can we ever show a hurting world the capital-T Truth if we never put that truth into practice?

Despite the fact that I didn't practice my piano lessons, it really is a gift to you all that I didn't grow up to be a piano-playing divorce lawyer. Thankfully, I have other gifts (at least I think so).

A Call within a Call

If I asked you to name one of the most compassionate people in history, nine times out of ten, Agnes Gonxha Bojaxhiu would be the answer. You're not familiar with that name? That's because we know her as Mother Teresa. Mother Teresa felt the call to a life of service as a twelve-year-old in Eastern Europe. Young Agnes left her home and family in 1928, never to see them again, to enter into a lifetime of service to God. As if becoming a nun wasn't a call enough, Mother Teresa felt "a call within a call" to serve the poorest of the poor in Calcutta, India. She established the Missionaries of Charity in 1950, with the mission of caring for the abandoned, hungry, sick, dying, and lepers. Compassion opened doors for Mother Teresa and the other sisters who joined her in the slums of India. She was able to show countless Hindus the love of Jesus simply by doing. Compassion was her greatest currency.

A decade after her death, a book was released that contained her personal letters to her superiors and confidants—letters she had later asked to be destroyed. Her request wasn't honored. In the book, *Mother Teresa: Come Be My Light*, the letters expose a side of the saintly woman the public had never seen or known. According to her letters, she felt alone and isolated and, at times, very far from and even abandoned by God. She once wrote in a letter, "Lord, my God, who am I that You should forsake me? The Child of your Love—and now become as the most hated one—the one—You have thrown away as unwanted—unloved. I call, I cling, I want—and there is no One to answer—no One on Whom I can cling—no, No One.—Alone. The darkness is so dark—and I am alone.—Unwanted, forsaken.—The loneliness of the heart that wants love is unbearable."*

---

* Mother Teresa, *Come Be My Light: The Private Writings of the Saint of Calcutta*, ed. Brian Kolodiejchuk (New York: Doubleday, 2007), Kindle edition.

The greatest example of compassion, Mother Teresa, who has inspired millions to selflessly serve others, proves to us that serving is not to be done alone. We are more effective in numbers. Mother Teresa experienced a deep loneliness, something that sounds very similar to compassion fatigue. We weren't made to reach the hurting alone.

There are many needs in our broken world. The need can be overwhelming, but we aren't called to carry the burden or fight every battle alone. There are causes that tug at my heart more than others, so those are the ones I apply myself to. Meanwhile, I champion those who give their time, energy, and resources to other causes.

Growing up in church, I thought the only way to really serve God was to be a missionary in Africa. One Saturday night as my mom was putting curlers in my hair while we watched *The Lawrence Welk Show* (our Saturday night family tradition), I wanted to impress my parents with my five-year-old spiritual maturity, so I told them God spoke to me and said I was going to be a missionary to Africa. Of course, my parents thought this was so adorable (and probably knew it wasn't true), but they obliged my tender heart and praised this revelation.

The next morning at church, my dad got up in front of the entire congregation and invited me to the pulpit to tell the church what God had told me. I was horrified because I had told them a complete lie, and now I had to get up in front of the entire church and lie again. I'd never been shy a day in my life until that moment. My dad had to pull the words out of my mouth until I finally announced that God had told me I was going to be a missionary to Africa. The congregation stood with cheers and applause, and I was convinced I was going straight to hell. I probably responded to every single salvation altar call for the next ten years after that in the attempt to be forgiven for my unpardonable sin. The irony, though, is that I did become a missionary, just not in Africa. I was a missionary in Washington, DC, and then later in Beverly Hills. I might not be a missionary to Africa, but God has certainly given me a mission field. And he has also given one to you. I encourage you to find your field because there's a world that needs you.

Are you wondering how you find your own field?

Ask yourself what breaks your heart. And I don't mean that you have momentary sadness and go on with your day. Rather, what truly makes your heart ache? It is something that you can't stop thinking about it, praying about, strategizing for. If absolutely nothing comes to mind, you have some work to do. And if a dozen different things come to mind, you have some work to do.

Compassion is the world's currency, the first crack in the door to someone's heart. When we show compassion, we're given the chance to tell people about Jesus and his love for them and show them our good, kind, caring God.

St. Francis of Assisi said it best: "Preach the gospel, and if necessary, use words." In a world that is so broken, so lost, and so desperately in need of comfort and hope, we have the greatest opportunity to preach the gospel by way of compassion.

Mother Teresa believed God gave her a call within a call to reach the desperately poor in Calcutta. She was already serving Jesus, but she heard an even deeper call that she could not shake.

What is your call within a call? Yes, you might already serve in your church or lead a Bible study or give to international missions. But what's your call within a call? Has God spoken to you about something and you keep putting it off for a later time? Your call within a call doesn't have to be living among the poor of India. It could be to love someone in your family who isn't so lovable. The Bible says, "Let your light shine before others, so that they may see your good works and give glory to your Father who is in heaven" (Matthew 5:16). One of the greatest ways to live out this verse is to love and respect the people closest to you.

In many ways, my call within a call is captured in the writing of this book. I realize empathy is not the hottest topic. People want to know how to live happier lives or how to overcome overwhelming trials. However, I've come to realize that one of the best ways to be happy or to get through an overwhelming trial is to love and encourage others.

My first prayer after Tennyson died was, "God, please don't let this all be for nothing. Bring purpose to this pain." After some time and a lot of healing, I leaned into that pain, and I have seen God use it exponentially for his purpose. I am a firm believer in the idea that God does not waste anything. Often the pain you have to walk through becomes a catalyst for your call within a call.

I don't know what your call within a call looks like, but I have a hunch you do. In fact, I would wager a bet that God is dropping a thought or creative idea into your heart right now. Sometimes we don't do the small things for the person around us because we think small is insignificant. But a bunch of small things add up to big things.

If we all did the small things, we could accomplish big things for God. The way compassion fatigue sets in, though, is when not enough people are doing the small things together, leaving a few to tackle the bigger things alone. God didn't create us to do anything alone. We're better and stronger together.

CHAPTER 7

The Art of Forgiveness

To be a Christian means to forgive the inexcusable because
God has forgiven the inexcusable in you.

—C. S. LEWIS

A few years before and after college, I lived in Washington, DC, just a few blocks from the U.S. Capitol, the Library of Congress, and the U.S. Supreme Court buildings. I spent hours in each of these magnificent buildings studying the architecture and learning about the history that was made in the very halls where I walked. I gazed at the countless artifacts and documents that have stood the course of time.

One of my favorite places to visit regularly was the Supreme Court. I had focused a lot of my undergraduate study on the Supreme Court and its historic cases, so it was quite exciting for me to learn even more from the actual hallowed courtrooms where these cases were argued. In fact, my senior thesis in college was on whether the Supreme Court's power was constitutional.

What's incredible to me is how accessible these buildings are to the public and they're all free admittance. Each place has a visitors' center with films describing the history and background of the building and the importance of what occurs in each place. Interesting tours provide even more details.

One part of the Court visitors' film, produced by C-Span in 1998, has always stood out to me and is something I reflect on when I find myself living or working among people I disagree with. The interviewer, Dick Howard, sat down with Chief Justice William Rehnquist and Associate Justices Sandra Day O'Connor, Stephen Breyer, and Clarence Thomas and asked them what they do first when they come into the room with one another. O'Connor, the first woman to be appointed to the Supreme Court, responded, "Shake hands, first thing." That statement has stayed with me because we can learn a lot from it as it relates to empathy. In her book *The Majesty of the Law*, O'Connor states that after some contentious rulings that the Court handed down in the early 2000s, it was noted that some of the nine justices weren't even speaking to one another. But they were forced to quickly rise above their differences. This is perhaps one of the reasons that Chief Justice Melville W. Fuller in the late nineteenth century instituted the customary "conference handshake," which has been a Court tradition ever since. Each day that the justices assemble to hear a case from the bench or join in private conference, at which they arrive at decisions, each justice shakes the hands of all of the other justices. Chief Justice Fuller believed the handshake showed "that the harmony of aims, if not views, is the court's guiding principle."

O'Connor went on to say in the C-Span film, "Every time we meet before we go on the bench or we have a conference, each justice shakes every other justice's hand. That's good. Because I think when you've touched someone's hand, you are less likely to hold a grudge, if you will, should we end up disagreeing on the merits of something."*

I love this tradition. No matter the difference of opinions, the justices keep their focus on their mutual mission: maintaining justice. They know that some of their colleagues may see the pathway to justice differently than they do, but nonetheless they respect one another's perspective. And it all starts with a handshake. Justice O'Connor quips, "It's difficult to shake hands without speaking."

This leads me to the important aspect of forgiveness as it relates to empathy: forgiveness struggles where there is no empathy. Empathy gives us the lens to see something from another person's point of view or perspective. This doesn't mean we have to agree with everyone; certainly we all know that the Supreme Court justices don't always agree with one another. But we must forgive in order to begin the next day with a genuine and respectful handshake. And in order to forgive, there must be a bit of humility and a lot of empathy.

---

* The Supreme Court Visitors' Film (C-span.org, February 16, 1998).

It's not easy, especially when someone has done something really awful to you.

I see two keys to forgiving. The first is to start small. My youth pastor while I was growing up used to ask, "How do you eat an elephant?" The answer, "Bite by bite." Can you imagine trying to forgive your spouse for infidelity when you never forgave your sister for losing your favorite shirt back in high school? I'm not saying that if you had forgiven your sister, forgiving your spouse now would be easy and automatic. Forgiveness is hard at any age and under any circumstance, but one way to make it easier is to start small.

It starts by forgiving the bad driver who cut you off on your way to work. Or by forgiving your friend who didn't invite you to a dinner party. Or by forgiving your boss for not giving you a promotion. In order for forgiveness to become natural to us, we have to start small and make it habitual.

The second key to forgiveness is getting a bigger perspective, or *God* perspective. Joseph of Genesis knew a thing or two about forgiving. In the story of Joseph, his older brothers were jealous of their father's favor with Joseph and wanted to kill him but instead settled for selling him to an Egyptian caravan.

Through a series of unpleasant events that followed, Joseph was convinced of God's providential protection and plan for his life. So years later, when Joseph was brought face-to-face with the brothers who betrayed him, he was able to look at them and say, "You meant evil against me, but God meant it for good" (Genesis 50:20). Essentially Joseph told his brothers, "Look, what you did was messed up. Unforgivable. But I choose to look at it from God's perspective and not my feeble, selfish, human heart." In that moment, Joseph forgave his brothers for their unthinkable actions.

As awesome as the story of Joseph is, I don't think he got to this place of forgiveness overnight. He had some rough years that developed him for that moment with his brothers.

After Joseph was sold to the caravan, he arrived in Egypt and was bought by Potiphar, an officer of Pharaoh. When Potiphar's wife falsely accused Joseph of raping her, he was thrown into prison for a crime he didn't commit—a lie and punishment he had to forgive.

As he sat in prison, he became acquainted with two men—Pharaoh's cupbearer and baker—with whom Pharaoh was displeased, so they were placed in prison. Both men began to have vivid dreams that Joseph was able to interpret. When the men were released, Joseph's one request in return for the interpretations was that they would remember him and mention him to Pharaoh. They forgot, another thing Joseph would have to forgive.

Several years later, the cupbearer remembered Joseph when Pharaoh was struggling to interpret dreams he was having. Joseph was brought before Pharaoh to interpret the man's dreams, and in gratitude, Pharaoh put Joseph in charge of his house.

Joseph understood something we all could benefit from: there's *always* a bigger picture and a process to consider, and when we keep our eyes on God's plan, even when we don't know what that plan is, we are better able to forgive. This is not easy to do. For many of us, forgiveness has been a tough area to fully surrender to God. But keeping a big-picture perspective helps; it's what kept Joseph's heart soft and able to forgive. Starting small and allowing God to give us a bigger perspective is the best way I know for how to live out forgiveness in my day-to-day life. I now know without a shadow of a doubt that I would not be writing this book if I had not walked through the painful experience of losing Tennyson. I know this for a couple of reasons. First, I would never have spent the last several years of my life studying empathy and learning from it. And second, the only reason I went to seminary to study the Bible and theology was my attempt not to hate God. I thought that if I studied the Bible, one of two things would happen: I would discover that all of this was a big cosmic joke and there is no loving and caring God, or I would discover that God is real, and even when life gets hard, he is with me and cares about every detail of my life. The latter was what I discovered. I love God's Word and all that it teaches us about his goodness and love, even in the midst of the worst of circumstances. When we look at our struggles from a different perspective, we allow ourselves the opportunity to turn that pain into something bursting with potential and purpose because God always wants to turn our pain into purpose.

Say It Again

A few months after Tennyson left this earth, I was not in good shape emotionally or physically. I was constantly ill and lost twenty pounds. I was anxious, never knew when a panic attack would strike, sick to my stomach, and exhausted all the time.

I made an appointment to see my doctor from when I was in college. I called him the "miracle worker" because he was the only doctor who was able to help my stomach issues then. Other doctors I consulted all inevitably said the same thing: "You need more fiber." But more fiber didn't help. Dr. Thornburg, however, discovered the root problem and gave me the appropriate natural medicine that this stressed-out college student needed. So when I found myself having stomach problems again, I made an appointment with my miracle worker.

Dr. Thornburg had me lie down on the table in his office just like every other time I had visited, but this time, instead of beginning the examination, he said, "Your mom told me what happened to your boyfriend. It wasn't your fault, you know." My sweet and caring mom had had an appointment with him earlier in the week and told him what had happened to Tennyson. Tears immediately poured down my face and onto the examination table. I quietly whispered, "I know." He then asked me something no one else had ever asked: "Have you forgiven him?"

What was difficult about Tennyson's death was the

mystery of it all. We are not completely sure what happened in his last moments on earth. Was it an accident? Was it intentional? These are questions I have to live with and perhaps never know the answers to. With little information, the police had ruled Tennyson's death a suicide. Those of us who knew him and loved him never wanted his death to overshadow his life and all the great things he did on this earth in his short years.

But when dealing with this type of tragedy, there is a dynamic of forgiving both the other person and yourself that is different from other types of deaths. I didn't have the whole story. I only knew that he was gone and my perspective was clouded with pain. I knew I had to try and see the situation from his perspective. That's what empathy does. It gives you a lens to look through that you would not normally have.

So in that moment when asked if I had forgiven him, my tears turned to uncontrollable sobs.

A few moments later, I was finally able to muster a screechy, "I don't know."

Dr. Thornburg let me lie there and cry for a few more moments until he interrupted the sobs and asked me if I would like to repeat a phrase after him. A little confused and hesitant about what this had to do with my stomach woes, I ultimately obliged and said, "Sure."

In his soft, kind voice Dr. Thornburg slowly said, "I forgive myself and others for all the wrong that has been done to me."

"Now repeat it after me, Tracy," he said. "I forgive myself and others for all the wrong that has been done to me."

With tears flowing and intermittent sobs, I reluctantly got it out: "I forgive myself and others for all the wrong that has been done to me."

"Say it again."

This time I said it with more power and control in my voice, "I forgive myself and others for all the wrong that has been done to me."

"Again."

"I forgive myself and others for all the wrong that has been done to me." I repeated the phrase a few more times until almost immediately I felt a release of what I can only describe as a balloon that popped.

I lay there a little longer until Dr. Thornburg broke the silence by asking, "How do you feel now?"

"Great," I replied. I was a little perplexed by what had just happened, but I really did feel completely fine.

Dr. Thornburg smiled and said, "Good. I'm glad," as he stood up to head to the door, meaning the appointment was over.

I interrupted his departure by asking, "So what do I need for my stomach?"

He turned back toward me from the door and said, "You will be fine now. You don't need anything."

A bit hesitant, I decided I trusted him enough not to argue, and I left.

As I drove away, I realized I did feel great. The sky was

bluer, the sun was brighter, and my life felt better. You know that feeling that comes when hope is restored. I had no idea that by not forgiving Tennyson for leaving me or not forgiving myself for all I had been holding myself responsible for was making me sick. Dr. Thornburg was right. I didn't need anything for my stomach, and those twenty pounds found their way back into my life. And that was okay because I was free from the weight of unforgiveness.

The *Mona Lisa*

Recently after finishing a ministry trip to Africa, I planned a three-day stop on my way home in one of my favorite cities, Paris. I had only one thing on my agenda to do during that three-day stay in the City of Lights: go to the Louvre and see Leonardo da Vinci's most famous masterpiece in person. After wandering the Louvre for hours and turning corner after corner of what felt more like a maze than an art museum, I stumbled into a large, bright room with dozens of incredible colors, landscapes, and impressive yet not-well-known pieces. In the middle of this grandiose room stood a makeshift wall with one very small portrait of a woman behind bulletproof glass next to guards where dozens upon dozens of people were desperately trying to catch a glimpse. It was nearly impossible to look above the crowd or get close enough to get a picture of the great *Mona Lisa* without pushing and shoving my way through the throng of bodies.

I had read and studied about this great work in art history class in college. We learned of da Vinci's unique and revolutionary painting technique and that it took him four years to finish the *Mona Lisa*. There has been much speculation about who the subject was and the reason for her slight smile in the portrait. Even Dan Brown's bestselling novel, *The Da Vinci Code*, has made the *Mona Lisa* a topic of many conspiracy theories. Millions of people come from around the world to see this famed piece of art, and I was thrilled to be one of them.

At best, it was one of the most underwhelming moments of my life, yet one of the most satisfying and unforgettable. I had imagined for years what the *Mona Lisa* in person would look like and how glorious I would feel to be standing in front of it, basking in its beauty. But the iconic painting was tiny and the room was crowded with other tourists, making it impossible to enjoy any basking since I had barely a moment to stand in front of the painting before I was pushed and elbowed aside.

I had expected much more.

This is, at times, how forgiveness feels to me. It can feel anticlimactic. Many times when I have made the conscious and biblical decision to forgive someone who has wronged, hurt, or betrayed me, I struggle and wrestle to get my heart in a position to follow through. By the time I do forgive the person, it feels as though life just moves on. I always think that if I'm going to forgive someone, there should at least be angels singing and some applause from heaven.

But it's more like Mona Lisa's smile: subtle and anticlimactic, but oddly and incredibly beautiful. My experience in the Louvre was not exactly the artistic epiphany that I had expected. I expected a quiet room with space and time to observe the brushstrokes and lighting and expression on Mona Lisa's delicate face. Still, as I was herded out of the room by the next rush of tourists, a strange sense of achievement rushed over me.

I did it.

I had seen one of the most renowned pieces of human creativity in history—and that is amazing.

Forgiveness never feels exactly like what I expect it to, but it is something I will never regret doing. There is a great sense of accomplishment for forgiving someone—not for accomplishment's sake but for *freedom*'s sake. Maybe heaven didn't sing when I forgave the person who deeply hurt me and maybe he didn't apologize to me like he should have, but my heart still feels light and free. It is that feeling that makes the process worth it.

If I had a dollar for every time I've heard someone (myself included) say, "I know I haven't forgiven her, but I'm not bitter," I'd be able to buy a new car. Maybe even two. The truth is, that just isn't possible. If you're withholding forgiveness from anyone, you are harboring bitterness, and it's just a matter of time until that bitterness becomes a giant chip on your shoulder and turns your heart to stone. Chips on your shoulder and a hardened heart sound a bit uncomfortable, and they are, so much so that they eventually become a prison.

So why do we need to forgive?

Because forgiveness is the key to freedom.

You can leave a legacy of forgiveness and empathy, or you can leave a legacy of bitterness and pain. It's your call—but everyone knows which one you chose because your life reflects it. Proverbs 27:19 (NIV) says it best: "As water reflects the face, so one's life reflects the heart." Our lives reflect our heart. Don't let a bitter heart be how the world sees you. Instead, be quick to forgive and move together toward sowing empathy to others.

Just as the daily handshakes between the Supreme Court justices help each rise above their differences, forgiveness is like starting a new narrative. It's shaking hands with someone you disagree with, has mistreated you, or said hurtful things about you. When you shake hands, you're walking toward empathy and recognizing that everyone has a perspective; you're choosing to understand someone from that person's vantage point. You may never agree with what he or she said about you or did to you, but you can always forgive.

Maybe literally shaking hands with someone is not feasible in your situation. Perhaps you don't live in the same city, state, or country. I suggest that our "shaking hands" tradition be that we pray for those who have hurt us, misused us, or spoken lies about us.

In one of the most famous passages in all of Scripture, Jesus admonishes us in his Sermon on the Mount to "love your enemies and pray for those who *persecute* you" (Matthew 5:44). Jesus can say this confidently because he's Jesus, but also because he goes on to do the very thing he commands us to do. In Luke 23:34, with the few breaths he had in him before dying on the cross, he prays, "Father, forgive them, for they know not what they do."

If Jesus can pray to the Father to forgive those who put him on a cross to die, then we can pray for those who have wronged us.

Have you ever tried to pray for someone you hate? It's not easy at first. In fact, it's like gritting your teeth and simply trying to get a few words out at first. When people ask me how they can forgive someone, the only answer I have is Matthew 5:44: love them and pray for them. It will become increasingly difficult to hate the person you pray for every day.

Forgiveness doesn't always feel spectacular, but it does lead to emotional and spiritual freedom, which is nourishment to a hardened heart.

CHAPTER 8

What to Say, What Not to Say

Any fool can know. The point is to understand.

—ALBERT EINSTEIN

Marte has known me my entire life. She was in Portland, Oregon, when I was born and was part of the church my parents led when my family moved to Boise, Idaho, when I was just a bubbly two-year-old. She moved to Boise not long after we did and has always acted as a second mom to me over the years. My siblings and I often stayed at her house when our parents went out of town. It was when I was staying with Marte once that I developed a fear of dogs.

I wasn't very old when it happened, and at this point the only dogs I had spent much time around were the farm dogs, Bo and Joe, on my grandparents' ranch. They couldn't be bothered too much by humans because they were taking long, lazy afternoon naps or chasing cars. But Marte's dogs were different: they were energetic and loved human contact. When my parents dropped me off at Marte's house on their way to the airport for a trip, I remember stepping out of the car and being knocked straight down to the ground by a HUGE dog. I was startled, crying, and scared to death of the big dog. Marte quickly scooped me up and comforted me, and out of the corner of my eye, I saw my mean older brother and sister laughing at what had just happened. I was afraid of that big, vicious dog until a few years later when I realized the dog wasn't big at all; in fact, he was tiny—probably about the same size as my little Andre Agassi is.

Marte and I have always gotten a kick out of that story.

Years later, Marte was still there to comfort me whenever I got hurt or was otherwise in need. She flew from Idaho to Colorado to support my family and me at Tennyson's memorial service, one of the toughest days of my life. I hadn't asked her to be there. I don't even remember exchanging that many words with her that day, but the ones we did meant the world to me. She told me, as she always had, that everything was going to be okay and that she was there for me. She was present. She made an effort to be there for me when I needed her the most. And I knew it and felt it and so appreciated that beautiful and active empathy.

The word *verbal* derives from a verb. And we all know from elementary English class that a verb shows action. Thus, I believe verbal empathy also shows action. It goes! It does! It shows up!

Empathy in action is saying something; it's being there for someone; it's tangible expressions of love; and it's committed for however long help is needed.

• • •

I have also been on the receiving end of *what not to say* moments. In the wake of Tennyson's death, many people around me were desperately trying to find the words to comfort me. And in some of their attempts to comfort, their words stung my open wound. I know now that that was not their intention; most people are truly trying to say what they think is the right thing. But that's the point: none of us have the answers to another person's pain. What we do have is the ability to be available and genuine. Our job in saying something is not to give a prescription for someone's difficult circumstances; it is simply to be present and to give comfort. I encourage anyone to resist the temptation to tell someone how to fix the situation. Instead, just listen, speak kind words of support, and listen some more.

A close friend told me, "At least this didn't happen after you and Tennyson were married and had children. That would have been really bad."

Yeah, 'cause this way is so much easier is how I would have *liked* to respond to that person. I had already thought through how I was grateful I was not a wife and mom grieving his death, but that was not a statement of comfort that I needed in that moment. What would have been more helpful was something like this: "I can't imagine how difficult this has been for you. I'm here for you."

The worst is when someone is grieving and, in our attempt to comfort her, we try to make a connection by saying,

"I know exactly how you feel . . ." Even if I *have* experienced a very similar loss as someone else, I avoid saying this at all cost. A better option might be to say, "I'm so sorry you are going through this. I can't imagine how much pain you feel, but I imagine it's really hard." Maybe further down the road, someone might ask about how you got through your situation; that is a perfect opportunity to open up and share all that you have learned on your journey. But until then, focus on comfort, not comparison.

Here are a few more *what not to say* statements that I think might be helpful for all of us as we practice empathy:

> *"You can still have another baby."*
> *"He is in a better place."*
> *"I know exactly how you feel."*
> *"There are so many worse things you could be going through."*
> *"She was just too good a person. God must have wanted her with him instead."*
> *"No one ever said life was fair."*
> *"Stop feeling sorry for yourself."*
> *"This is what happens when you make bad decisions."*

Here are a few suggestions (but not an exhaustive list) of *what to say:*

> *"I am so sorry for your loss."*
> *"You're not alone."*
> *"I wish I had the right words to comfort you; just know I care."*

"You are important to me."

"How are you doing today?" (Grievers live one day at a time.)

"May I give you a hug?"

"We're going to get through this."

"How can I be praying for you today [this week]?"

"Is there something I can do for you today?"

"Here is my number. I want you to call me at any time, day or night, if you need anything."

"I don't know how you feel, but I am here to help you in any way."

"My favorite memory of your loved one is . . ."

"I stand with you in your grief. You are not alone."

It's tough to know exactly what to say to someone who is going through an unimaginable experience. In fact, you don't need to have the answers, so don't beat yourself up for not knowing exactly what to say in a moment of crisis. Don't run away from someone who is hurting because you're not sure your words can comfort. Instead, choose to say something that makes the person who is hurting feel your connection to their pain. The author and poet Maya Angelou famously said, "People will forget what you said, people will forget what you did, but people will never forget how you made them feel."* When we are faced with the task to say

---

* Maya Angelou, quoted in Bob Kelly, *Worth Repeating: More Than 5,000 Classic and Contemporary Quotes* (Grand Rapids, MI: Kregal Publications, 2003), 263.

something to someone in pain, may our words leave people feeling loved, comforted, and surrounded in their greatest time of need.

Silence Is Deadly

It was a few years after Tennyson's death, and I was doing pretty well. I was starting to feel like my old self again. I decided to go to a church conference and was excited to see a lot of old friends I hadn't seen for a while. I had been avoiding gatherings like these in order to ward off any awkward or hurtful moments, which seemed to accompany such events.

During the first evening session of the conference, I noticed a few people I had known most of my life were acting a little sheepish around me. They hadn't come to greet me the way they normally would and seemed to be avoiding eye contact with me, so I decided not to approach them either. As the conference went on, I found myself in a hallway with one of these old friends who had seemed to be avoiding me the past couple of days. Finally, she approached me and, with tears in her eyes, said, "I never knew what to say to you after Tennyson died. I've never known anyone who has had to go through anything like this." I looked at her and said, "I know. I'd never known anyone who had to go through anything like this either."

It was in that moment I realized many of the people who loved me and cared for me didn't mean to be silent; they just didn't know what to say. But what they didn't realize is that their silence broke my heart even more than it already was. I realized that saying something not only was the antidote for their awkwardness, it was also the antidote for someone feeling as if he or she is walking alone through a hardship.

With several years since Tennyson's death behind me, I didn't remember all the awkward or insensitive things people said to me, but I have not forgotten the impact of the meaningful people in my life who said nothing. Some of them may have reached out to my parents or siblings to relay a message. And perhaps years later, when they felt the discomfort had lifted, they would try to act as though nothing had happened, but at the time, they rarely acknowledged my pain.

I think many of us want to say something to those who are facing a challenge, but out of fear of saying the wrong thing, we settle for silence. You may disagree with me, but taking the risk of saying the wrong thing might be better than saying nothing. It was the silence of my friends that wounded my sensitive soul more than the trivial words from some well-intended acquaintances.

If I can encourage you to do anything in the wake of a friend or loved one's grief or pain of any kind, it is to say *something*. Silence feels like adding death unto death. Hurting people aren't looking for you to have all the answers;

they just want to know they are not alone. I know I just wanted to feel surrounded.

Silence is cold and lonely. Comforting words are like a warm blanket in the middle of a blizzard.

Silence as it relates to empathy can also come from the griever. We might send someone a card or text message, leave a voice mail, or drop off a meal—and hear nothing back. Here you are selflessly pouring out your heart, time, and energy to someone and . . . nothing. I think this is another reason we don't extend empathy in the first place. There is an expectation of appreciation and gratitude in return, and when we don't get it, our feelings get hurt and we decide not to go down that road again.

Please don't go there. Decide to show empathy and then leave it there. In order for empathy to be genuine and authentic, we can't expect a response.

Those who are hurting are feeling overwhelmed by their grief and pain. This is the time for them to be covered by your grace and be excused from normal protocol. When you show empathy—when you're doing as Jesus commanded—your reward will come from God, not the person you're giving your love to. And his rewards are beyond compare. But there is one thing I will add and can assure you of from my own experience: even if the person doesn't respond, know within your heart that he or she is grateful.

The same is true for those on the receiving end of empathy. Don't let yourself get hurt or run narratives through your head as to why someone said this or someone else did that. Whenever we're going through high-stress situations, our emotions are heightened and we can tend to be more sensitive. Trust that people care about and love you; maybe they haven't reached out to you because they aren't sure how or they don't know what to say.

Putting our hope and healing in the hands of other people is always a risky idea. We are all fallible creatures, and people are bound and destined to disappoint us. So we can hope that something doesn't happen or we can hope something does happen. We can hope someone says the right thing, or we can hope *we* don't say the wrong thing. We can hope our team wins the Super Bowl, or we might hope we don't lose our job. But here is some reassurance for those hope-weary minds: the biblical definition of *hope* is not a hope-so but a *know*-so. Our hope in God is surer than the sun rising in the morning.

Remember those Psalms I mentioned previously? So often they are a sweet blend of the entire spectrum of emotions—of thanksgiving, praise, and lament. And many of them end with the same conclusion: "I have put my hope in your word" (Psalm 119:74 NIV), "I have put my hope in your word" (Psalm 119:81 NIV), and "In his word I put my hope" (Psalm 130:5 NIV). That's why, like this Psalm put it, "It is better to take refuge in the Lord than to trust in humans" (Psalm 118:8 NIV). Our trust is in God, not people. In fact,

Psalm 13 (the lament Psalm of David we looked at a few chapters back) has a pretty spectacular finish. "But I trust in your unfailing love; my heart rejoices in your salvation. I will sing the Lord's praise, for he has been good to me" (Psalm 13:5–6 NIV).

So put your hope and trust in a God that will not fail you.

And choose to believe the best in your friends and their words. Choose to extend grace. Choose to understand the fact that they and you will fail. Choose to put your ultimate faith in something much bigger, because by doing so, you're actively participating in empathy.

No Need to "Get Over It"

Recently at church I was talking to a wonderful woman who had lost her husband suddenly. He had been the picture of health: strong, healthy, and active. In fact, he was working out when he had a sudden, fatal heart attack. The shock that family experienced is unimaginable. Rebecca, his widow, and I were talking about grief, and she thanked me for being open about my experience with loss. I listened to her as she told me, with tears in her eyes, how long it has been since he passed away and how she and her two daughters have navigated the treacherous road of their grief. I asked her what has been one of the more challenging aspects of grief and she mentioned it's difficult when others are "over it" and expect her to just be over it by then too.

This broke my heart. It had been only two and a half years since she had lost her partner, best friend, father to her children, and grandfather to their grandbabies. Not everyone can "get over" their loss on someone else's timetable. That is the antithesis to empathy.

Two years after Tennyson's passing, people started setting me up on dates. When you're the last single person among your family and friends, it somehow becomes their unsolicited duty to marry you off. And the setups over the years have been legendary. Oh, the stories I have . . .

One time a couple told me they wanted me to meet a guy they knew and loved. I told them no, politely but firmly. I was not interested in him even though he seemed like a nice person. I just knew he wasn't a good fit for me. Nevertheless, this couple went behind my back and began organizing their clandestine operation. Before I knew it, I was involved in a relationship I did not feel good about, and it didn't take long for it to be apparent to everyone that it was not working.

My heart had become collateral damage in a matchmaking gone badly. Weeks later when I was still processing the situation, the couple who had set it up asked how I was doing. I told them I was sad and trying to work through it. Both of them separately but on the same day told me, "You just need to get over it."

I couldn't believe my ears. Not only was I trying to process the pain of the situation, but now I was also hurting from their words: "Get over it." Get over the situation they helped put me in? They just as easily could've shot me or stabbed me in the back; I was convinced it must feel the same. I was shocked and numbed by their callous words. I knew I had to take responsibility for my part (I agreed to meet the man in the first place) and not hold my hurt against them. I had to extend the grace I spoke about earlier. I am accountable for my own decision not to lash back or bear a grudge. But to tell me to "get over it" was not helpful. After some long, deep breaths (to keep me from saying what I really wanted to say to them), many prayers, and several sessions with my counselor, I realized that these people were not horrible; they were people who lacked understanding as well as empathy. It's pretty amazing what horrible things will come out of a not-so-horrible person's mouth when those two ingredients are missing. I'm sure they didn't mean for their advice to come out the way I received it, but it hurt all the same. And although the words from my friends were hurtful and unhelpful, I had just as much responsibility to show grace and forgiveness in return.

Ephesians 4 sandwiches compassion and forgiveness together as if to say these go hand in hand: "Be kind and compassionate to one another, forgiving each other, just as in Christ God forgave you" (Ephesians 4:32). The apostle Paul is instructing readers to start with kindness and compassion toward those who may have hurt them, followed by forgiveness. Jesus is the ultimate example in every single situation. If he could empathize with and forgive us, we can do the same toward others.

I had to let go of the pain of those words, "get over it." The reality is that most of us don't know *what to say and what not to say*. And when I was honest with myself and acknowledged that I haven't always said the right thing in every situation, how could I expect others to? I can't and I shouldn't, so I won't. Instead, I'm going to practice grace in those moments when someone else isn't extending me the same courtesy.

Tangible Empathy

The simplest actions can leave the biggest impact. This was especially true for me in my processing of grief. Some of the simplest gestures propelled me in unexplainable ways.

When Sally bought me a beautiful checkered coat, I felt beautiful again.

When Caroline gave me my first pair of diamond earrings, I felt value and worth again.

When Robin wrote me a card full of scripture verses, I felt God's love and promises rush over me at a time when I had no energy or motivation to read my Bible.

To each of these women, these actions probably seemed small and insignificant in relation to my surmounting grief, but to me, their gifts meant the world. Sometimes a gift, whether it's a simple card or diamond earrings, is a way to live out tangible empathy in action.

Remember when I was bawling in the middle of Barnes &

Noble? I was ready to give up on God. I was worried that the pain I was feeling would never leave. I was afraid I would never be happy again. I believed my life was worthless and completely hopeless. Yet suddenly my phone beeped. I looked down and saw a text message from a number I did not recognize. The number was not in my contacts so I was unsure of who this text was from.

I opened the text and saw that it was from a pastor who was a friend of our family. He had heard the news of my loss while he was ministering in South America, got my number, and sent me a text to tell me he was so sorry to hear about my tragic loss. In the text, he told me he was preaching at a church and had the whole congregation pray for me. He reiterated that he and his family would do anything for me. All I had to do was ask.

I will never forget how that text message from Pastor Tommy made me feel. I wasn't alone in that Barnes & Noble after all. If someone I did not even know that well could take the time to send me a message while out of the country, then how much more did God care about me?

It was in that moment that I realized that the art of empathy doesn't mean having all the answers. It just means demonstrating to the brokenhearted God's unfailing love. Perhaps this is the very reason God created community: for empathy to shine.

CHAPTER 9

Generous Mercy

I think we all have empathy. We may not have enough courage to display it.

—MAYA ANGELOU

The first week my new roommate, Keila, moved into my house, she contracted the swine flu, also known as the H1N1 influenza virus. Basically, swine flu is a really, really bad case of the flu. Her first few weeks in her new home consisted of her lying on the couch with a fever, body aches, chills, and a cough and feeling pretty much like death was near.

I'm kind of a hypochondriac, minus the "kind of" part. The moment I start experiencing any unusual symptoms in my body, I do what every mature and faith-filled Christian should do: Google my symptoms on WebMD, immediately followed by calling my mom and informing her of my self-diagnosis, to which she responds by talking me down off the ledge of impending death. My family finally banned me from searching WebMD because every time I got sick,

WebMD and I decided my days were numbered and quickly coming to a close.

WebMD is dangerous because the negative information can play tricks with your mind. All you have to do is type your symptoms—headache, sore throat, eye twitch, and bruise—and you'll receive pages of details that can put you in panic overdrive. You might as well accept the fact right then that you are going to die sooner than you had anticipated. I think Satan might be the creator and CEO of WebMD because it is pure joy to him to create such panic and fear in all of us hypochondriacs of the world. In all fairness, I have heard of people who have actually used WebMD to recognize a dire condition and go to their health care provider, which likely saved their life. Maybe Satan didn't invent WebMD after all, but I'm still banned from it.

You can only imagine how I do around someone who is infectiously sick. If "not great," "terrible," or "horrible" comes to your mind, you are absolutely correct. To be fair, I'm only awful with people whose sickness is contagious. My brother has type 1 diabetes, and I have been stellar in crisis moments with him. When he was having a dangerously low blood sugar attack while we were driving in a city I was unfamiliar with and no amount of glucose tabs or juice was able to bring his sugar up, I was somehow calm and able to get him to a hospital where they stabilized his blood sugar and saved his life. Blood and needles don't bother me either. When my brother had his appendix and gallbladder taken out just weeks apart, I stayed with him at the hospital and helped him clean his infected incision (which was the most disgusting thing I have ever seen, but I assured him it wasn't gross at all; he totally bought it).

Hospitals don't bother me either. I have spent countless hours in hospitals visiting and praying with patients. So maybe I'm not a hypochondriac as much as I am a germaphobe. What have we learned about me? If you're in the hospital and blood is shooting out everywhere, call me and I'll be there, but if you get the swine flu and are lying helpless on a couch, I won't come within ten feet of you.

Poor Keila. She was helpless and miserable, and the best I could offer was to run to the drugstore to get the medicine she needed to feel better. I would get up in the middle of the night when she was sleeping and disinfect the entire house to ensure that I would not contract her awful ailment. The worst part was that one night when I desperately wanted to get out of the contaminated house, I backed right into Keila's car as I was hurrying to leave. So not only was she dying on the couch; now she also had a huge dent in her cute little Mini Cooper.

If I have learned anything about empathy, it is that it often challenges my conveniences and preferences. Otherwise, we would all probably be great at showing love and compassion to our world . . . every single second. For me, showing empathy to Keila was way out of my comfort zone and preference. Give me a hurt dog lying on the side of the road, someone choking in a restaurant, or a mother who just lost her son. But someone with the flu—not my cup of tea.

Early Christians

I'm not sure I would have been a very good Christian in the first and second centuries if I couldn't even help my ailing roommate. In fact, the verdict is still out as to whether I am a very good twenty-first-century Western Christian.

The mantra of the early Christians was to identify themselves as a Christian first and foremost; everything they did came out of this reality. Their actions had to be congruent with the life and teachings of Jesus. This fact has often been erased from our current culture.

We know from history and our reading of the Gospels that diseases plagued the ancient world. According to Rodney Stark in his book *The Triumph of Christianity*, smallpox devastated and killed tremendous numbers of people, from the crowded and overpopulated cities of the Roman Empire to the rural towns on the outskirts. Overpopulation, filth, lethal plagues, and disease overtook the Roman Empire, and the dead and dying were thrown into the streets.

Stark argues that compassion and mercy were regarded as character flaws, and mercy was considered as providing unearned relief, which in that age was contrary to justice.[*] In their minds, mercy was reserved for those who *deserved* it. This decline of love and mercy was the defining philosophy of the ancient world. And yet Christianity thrived in this

---

[*] Rodney Stark, *The Triumph of Christianity* (New York: HarperCollins, 2011), 112.

moral climate as it taught and lived out mercy, giving relief even to those who didn't "deserve" it—whatever that means.

Mercy was also exhibited through fearless generosity in the face of death or at the risk of their reputation. When plague overtook the Roman Empire, killing a third of the population, the goal was to avoid anyone who was sick or showed any signs of sickness.[*] That meant that anyone who showed symptoms was thrown in the streets to die alongside the piles of bodies that had already been abandoned. It was the fearless early Christians who sacrificed their own health and wealth to care for the sick and dying. Christians of that day felt it was their responsibility to care, and not just for other believers but for strangers and outsiders as well. When no one else would sacrifice their life, Christians would.[†]

Sounds a lot like giving yourself away.

Sounds a lot like martyrdom of the soul.

Early Christianity taught that compassion and mercy were qualities that all believers must operate in. Since God is kind, merciful, and compassionate, all Christians should live out these same virtues. These early Christians took seriously the new commandment Jesus gave His disciples in the Gospel of John: "A new commandment I give to you, that you love one another: just as I have loved you, you also are to love one another. By this all people will know that

---

[*]   Stark, *The Triumph of Christianity*, 114.

[†]   Ibid., 112

you are my disciples, if you have love for one another" (John 13:34–35). They believed it was their mission to show the world God's love and mercy—just as God had been so loving and merciful to them.

The first Christian community in history is recorded in the book of Acts, and it is one of the most outstanding views of what generous mercy should look like. It's in this book that Peter preached the sermon of his life. After he finished speaking, the crowd wanted this powerful life they could have with Jesus, so Peter told them to repent and be baptized in the name of Jesus. Peter was apparently quite convincing because the Bible records that about three thousand souls did just that. Immediately there was a large community of Jesus followers and, *bam*, the Capital-C Church began.

In the closing verses of Acts 2, we get a taste of what this first church looked like, and it is beautiful:

And they devoted themselves to the apostles' teaching and the fellowship, to the breaking of bread and the prayers. And awe came upon every soul, and many wonders and signs were being done through the apostles. And all who believed were together and had all things in common. And they were selling their possessions and belongings and distributing the proceeds to all, as any had need. And day by day, attending the temple together and breaking bread in their homes, they received their food with glad and generous hearts, praising God and having favor with

all the people. And the Lord added to their number day by
day those who were being saved. (Acts 2:42–47, emphasis
mine)

They had all things in common. It sounds to me that
everyone was walking in empathy and understanding with
one another.

This has got to be utopia!

Or heaven!

Everyone has everything in common? It's a far cry from
society today, don't you think? I can't fathom a world like
that. It doesn't even seem possible—but it was and it is. Impossible things become possible when we truly encounter
God and put his ways first in life.

Empathy has the power to create not just personal
change but social change. Humanity hasn't always had
everything in common, because if it did, God wouldn't
have highlighted this reality in the Bible. Empathy re-
moves the prejudice and classes and evens the playing
field. There is no right way or wrong. No smart or dumb.
Good or bad. The Christians in the early church were
simply looking to God instead of themselves—all together in unison, the way musicians in an orchestra look
at their conductor.

I believe Acts 2:44 is a beautiful picture of how God
wants his church to look today. It is a picture of society built
on self-giving love, not self-taking interest.

Elie Wiesel, a Holocaust survivor, wrote *Night*, about his

horrific experience as a teenager with his father in the Nazi concentration camps at Auschwitz and Buchenwald. Wiesel was awarded the Nobel Peace Prize in 1986 and devoted much of his life to the mission of human rights. Wiesel once famously said, "The opposite of love is not hate, it's indifference."

Perhaps our worst problem is not hate, but rather apathy. We just don't care. This is quite different from what we see in the early church. They believed in God, they cared about each other in the truest form, and they held all things in common.

I believe that the reason many Christians and churches fail to look like Acts 2 today is not because God performed miracles only in "the Bible days"; I think it's because our Western way of thinking has taught us to fit God into our beliefs rather than believing in God and letting him change our beliefs, thinking, opinions, and agendas.

Nevertheless, many amazing churches around the world today operate similarly to the Acts 2 church. The first time I visited the Dream Center in Los Angeles, I was a young, naive high school student from Idaho. The Dream Center is a church dedicated to helping drug addicts, gang members, AIDS victims, the homeless, and so many more hurting people who receive spiritual and physical support. We took food, water, and hope to the homeless of Skid Row. We painted an entire floor of the Dream Center so men, women, and children could have a place to live. We cleaned houses and raked leaves one Saturday morning with the center's

Adopt-a-Block program. We sat in Bible study and prayed for people who were overcoming addictions and learning to walk with Jesus. The vision of Pastors Tommy and Matthew Barnett to start the Dream Center is an accurate expression of what Acts 2 could look like today.

Christine Caine's vision, along with that of Hillsong Church, is to eradicate human trafficking in the twenty-first century through the A21 Campaign, another great example of what Acts 2 looks like.

Anytime we see a church participating in active missionary work—feeding the hungry, giving drink to the thirsty, welcoming the strangers, clothing the naked, visiting the sick and those in prison—we see a church doing the work of God.

This generous living we see in Acts 2:45 (ESV)—"they were selling their possessions and belongings and distributing the proceeds to all, as any had need"—is profound because most of them had scant possessions of their own, and yet they still gave. Pure and sincere generosity is not a character trait or a virtue of a really, really good person; it is the expression of a heart that fully believes in God and has been filled with his spirit. God blesses us so that we can be a blessing. He does not simply bless us just so we can be blessed. God's generosity toward us is so that we can be generous with others.

One sure way to feel frustrated and empty in life is to be stingy and give small. Proverbs 11:24 (NET) says, "One person is generous and yet grows more wealthy, but another withholds more than he should and comes to poverty." The great paradox of the Christian way is that generosity is a determining factor for prosperity in God's economy. Living generously leads to every kind of happiness because generous living is the most like Jesus we can be.

I'm not just referring to generosity with money. Giving money can be a big part of it, but that's not all of it. Generous living also includes giving basics such as food, clothing, shelter, ideas, time, and energy: you have to give something away that is yours in order to be generous. When you give something of yourself, especially when it takes sacrifice—meaning that it takes you out of your comfort zone—you lose a part of yourself. That's what it means to be like Jesus.

Jesus' entire life was shaped by giving himself away.

Matthew 16:24 (ESV) reiterates what it takes to be a follower of Jesus. We saw this a little earlier from Mark's gospel, but the words bear repeating: "Then Jesus told his disciples, 'If anyone would come after me, let him *deny* himself and take up *his cross* and follow me.'"

To *deny himself* in the Greek means to "deny utterly or disown." It is also believed to mean, "to forget one's self, lose sight of one's self and one's own interests."* What?! Forget all my interests? That's enough to make me hesitate and think twice. And yet it gets worse before it gets better.

Not only must we disown our self and interests; the verse goes on to say, "and take up *his cross* and follow me."

---

* Joseph H. Thayer, *Thayer's Greek-English Lexicon of the New Testament* (Peabody, MA: Hendrickson Publishers, 1997), 54.

Cross here in the Greek is "an upright stake," which signified the most cruel punishment in ancient times. The Romans had perfected the art of death on the cross for the worst of criminals. Yet Jesus, who was innocent, experienced this excruciating way to die. *Take up your cross* in Matthew's gospel illustrates that in order to follow Jesus and truly serve others, there must be a death of something in us that is similar to the death that Jesus experienced through his crucifixion.

This is why Paul said in Galatians 2:20a (ESV), "I have been *crucified* with Christ. It is no longer I who live, but Christ who lives in me." The word *crucified* here in the Greek means "to crucify together with." According to *Thayer's Greek-English Lexicon*, it means, "By the death of the cross I have become utterly estranged from (dead to) my former habit of feeling and action."* Hence, *to be crucified* was a big statement for Paul, especially since many Romans in the first century wouldn't even use the word *cross* or *crucifixion*. The reality of this brutal but common form of death conjured up real and vivid imagery of the most atrocious way to die in the ancient world.

However, when the apostle Paul writes, "I have been crucified with Christ," it begs the question as to what the ancient world must have thought.

Crucified? Paul sounds crazy. He has never experienced the betrayal, ridicule, excruciating pain, or death that ac-

---

* Ibid., 608.

companies the crucifixion that Jesus endured. How can he say, "I have been crucified with Christ"?

Eugene Peterson said, "Crucifixion ends one way of life and opens up another."* "Being crucified with Jesus" means the end of a life that is centered around our favorite pronouns—*me*, *myself*, and *I*—and opens a life that is centered on God and his plan for us.

When we identify with the crucifixion of Jesus, we lose our self-centeredness. We even lose the memory of who we once were and accept a brand-new identity in Jesus Christ.†

This is how the early Christians and the Church of Acts could live out such generous and authentic empathy. They lost themselves and found Jesus.

Paul-itics

I am proud to be an American. I love the stars and stripes and all that they represent. I don't appreciate when someone says something negative about the *amber waves of grain* or *purple mountains majesty*. I get emotional when I hear the national anthem or when I see one of our war veterans. I love to exercise my right to vote, and I proudly wear my

---

* Eugene H. Peterson, *Traveling Light: Modern Meditations on St. Paul's Letter of Freedom* (Colorado Springs: Helmers & Howard Publishers, 1988), 76.
† Tom Wright, *Paul for Everyone: Galatians and Thessalonians* (London: Society for Promoting Christian Knowledge, 2002), 25.

"I voted" sticker. The Fourth of July is my favorite holiday (well, it's at least tied with Christmas). I get chills from the pomp and circumstance at parades, reenactments, and historical documentaries telling about the sacrifices made in the past so I can experience freedom today. Don't even get me started when our military does a flyover at the start of a football game: I get so overcome with emotion, I want to chant "USA, USA, USA!" It's difficult for me to accept losing to any other country in the Olympics (summer or winter) EVER. I love when we dominate the Olympic medal count, and I don't feel bad about it one bit. I think America is the greatest country in the world because it is the nation I was born in—the country God placed me in for better or for worse. It will forever be my first and foremost mission field for winning others to Jesus.

I love this country.

I'm a patriot.

Where I have to be careful, like a lot of other patriots, is not to drift into a form of hypernationalism. Nationalists are nation first, everything else second. This is a predicament for Christians, because we are taught to be Christian first, and everything else second. See the potential conflict?

Being a Christian does not mean demeaning or disrespecting our country or your nationality. It also doesn't mean loving your national, political, and social identities more than your spiritual one in Christ.

Paul addresses this dilemma quite a bit throughout the New Testament. In Colossians, he writes, "Here there is no

Greek and Jew, circumcised and uncircumcised, barbarian, Scythian, slave, free; but Christ is all, and in all" (Colossians 3:11). In Galatians, Paul makes the same point again: "There is neither Jew nor Greek, there is neither slave nor free, there is no male and female, for you are all one in Christ Jesus" (Ephesians 3:28).

Ethnic, social, national, and gender distinctions were second to the reality of being in the family of God. In other words, to Paul, you were a Christian first and everything else was second. These Christians of the ancient world would likely struggle to understand if I, today, identified myself as part Dutch, one-eighth Swedish, and Scottish before anything else. Or if I stated I am American from the state of Idaho first. Or I am just a woman living in a man's world first. To the Christians of the ancient world and to the Christians of today, we are first and foremost followers of Jesus. We are Christians.

Ethnocentrism has become a dominant problem in the Western world. This word comes from the Greek *ethno* meaning "people" and *centric* meaning "center." This belief fosters the right to put one's own people group above every other people group, whether it is race or residency. It is a superiority mind-set that "my people" and "my beliefs" are greater than anyone else's. This is the very thing Jesus came to demolish.

In Matthew 20:28 we see that Jesus' mission on earth was for others, "even as the Son of Man came not to be served but to serve, and to give his life as a ransom for many" (ESV). Jesus came to give himself away. Everything he did was for others. The example Jesus gives us is the exact opposite of individualism, radical nationalism, or ethnocentrism. When it comes to Jesus, it's *others* first. Putting others first is the way to empathy. Can you imagine how quickly cultural divides would end and cultural memory would heal if everyone (every side, every opinion, every tradition of the past) decided, "you first"? Empathy does this. It is the great equalizer for human harmony.

Love in Action

Does this kind of Christian action and empathy sound a lot like love?

> *Love is patient and kind; love does not envy or boast; it is not arrogant or rude. It does not insist on its own way; it is not irritable or resentful; it does not rejoice at wrongdoing, but rejoices with the truth. Love bears all things, believes all things, hopes all things, endures all things.* (1 Corinthians 13:4–7)

1 Corinthians 13 was never intended to be the modern poetic prose we recite at weddings or the passage of Scripture we quote when one of our loved ones is rude, arrogant, or insists on his own way. Paul likely wrote this to remind the church of Corinth that what we do, we do in love because it will have the greatest impact for good. Love garners the greatest attention for Christ.

The Greek word for love in 1 Corinthians 13 is *agape*.

Agape means goodwill, charity, and benevolence. It was not a word used very often before the New Testament. One might find this Greek word only twenty or so times in other writings. But it was a fitting word for the Christian love Paul is describing. *Agape* is found 116 times throughout the New Testament. Seventy-five of those uses are by Paul.*

The apostle Paul points out in this love chapter that agape is not an emotion; it is an action. In other words, empathy is love in action, the sine qua non of the Christian story. It's who we are. It's how we're called to live.

The Christian story is and has always been about generous love and mercy. Today the needs in our world might look different, but the call to action is the same.

Is He Safe?

What is the point of life if it's not a big, sometimes scary, generous adventure of giving yourself away? We've conditioned ourselves into believing Christianity is the safe path. We safeguard our lives like we kid-proof our homes. Instead of covering electrical sockets, we refrain from speaking to people who are different from us—stranger danger.

We naturally lean toward safety, especially as we get

---

* Leon Morris, *Tyndale New Testament Commentaries: 1 Corinthians*, vol. 7 (Downers Grove, IL: Intervarsity Press, 1985).

older. I get it. I do it too. In my teenage years, I would jump off a cliff into the water below without a second of hesitation. Now, years later, I hesitate and make a pro-and-con list in my head as to whether it's a good idea. I search for statistics by quickly Googling ("How many people have died jumping off a cliff into water?") before I make my decision. Following Jesus is often an uncomfortable place, yet it's the safest place you can ever be. Showing empathy to a stranger means living out a mission, and mission fields often scare us.

Remember the great classical fiction series *The Chronicles of Narnia* by C. S. Lewis? My siblings and I probably read *The Lion, the Witch and the Wardrobe* a dozen times. My grandparents had a farmhouse a hundred miles from where I grew up, and I spent a portion of my summers there each year. The upstairs of the farmhouse had two bedrooms, which were the bedrooms of my mom and her sister when they were growing up. My grandma kept all my mom's old Barbies, other dolls, and toys in her room for me to play with. She even saved my mom's old cowboy hat and boots, so I pretended and dreamed of becoming a rodeo queen. I'm still a little devastated this dream was never realized.

A huge adjoining closet with sliding doors divided the two upstairs bedrooms. I would enter the closet from one room and exit into the other room and imagine I had entered into the magical and mystical Kingdom of Narnia just like Peter, Susan, Edmund, and Lucy did. I would pretend I was exploring the magnificent, yet scary, snowy new world that was caught under the White Witch's spell. I would converse with the animals on my grandparents' ranch like they were Mr. and Mrs. Beaver or Tumnus of Narnia. The dogs, cats, horses, and cows were less engaging than the creatures of Narnia, but my imagination didn't need their cooperation. I would navigate through the creeks, pastures, and huge trees of the ranch in search of Aslan. Since we all knew he was "on the move," I pretended to eat gobs and gobs of Turkish delight. I mean, how great did Turkish delight sound from the book? Years later while I was in London, I stumbled on the Narnia treat in a bakery and couldn't wait to taste it. But I was unpleasantly surprised. Let's just say it was one thing better left to the imagination than to reality.

In the actual story, the four children—Peter, Susan, Lucy, and Edmund—keep hearing that Aslan is on the move, that he will make the world right and overturn the White Witch's power. This leads to a powerful dialogue where Susan and Lucy ask who this Aslan is.

> "Is, is he a man?" asked Lucy.
>
> "Aslan a man!" said Mr. Beaver sternly. "Certainly not. I tell you he is King of the wood and the son of the great emperor-beyond-the-sea. Don't you know who is the King of the Beasts? Aslan is a lion—the Lion, the great lion."
>
> "Ooh!" said Susan, "I'd thought he was a man. Is he, quite safe? I shall feel rather nervous about meeting a lion."
>
> "That you will, dearie, and no mistake," said Mrs. Beaver; "if there's anyone who can appear before Aslan without their knees knocking, they're either braver than most or else just silly."

"Then he isn't safe?" said Lucy.

"Safe?" said Mr. Beaver; "don't you hear what Mrs. Beaver tells you? Who said anything about safe? 'Course he isn't safe. But he's good. He's the King, I tell you."

Just as in this dialogue one of our greatest obstacles in following Jesus isn't that we don't want to, but rather that we're afraid to. We don't want to be asked to do something we are afraid of. What exactly are we afraid of? Usually it's something that will make us uncomfortable.

We want to believe that following God is synonymous with living a safe, comfortable life. Yet most of the time, being a Christian is rarely comfortable.

It's not a life that is promised to be problem free, but it is a life promised to be connected to what God is doing. And everything God is doing is good!

Being in a place that scares you doesn't mean you are in the wrong place or without God. It might actually mean you are in the exact place God wants and needs you to be.

What is the thing that scares you? For some, it may be a new place God wants to send you. For others, it may mean going to Pakistan. For others, it may mean living out love toward your next-door neighbor. Or perhaps building an orphanage scares you, but you can't shake thinking about it; that might be what God is sending you to do. Or maybe your boss keeps popping up in your prayers and you know you are to step out in boldness and ask if she needs prayer for anything. But it scares you to death, which might mean that is exactly where God is sending you. Or perhaps you know you are supposed to run for political office but are terrified by the thought. Maybe it's the exact place God is sending you. Or maybe it's the thought of showing someone mercy when we think that person should get what he deserves instead—perhaps that's what scares us. And quite possibly, it is the place of mercy that God is sending us.

All I know is I haven't done enough that scares me yet. I want to be more like those early Christians. I want God to come and change my whole life, my whole heart, and my whole mind.

Goodness knows, plenty of Christians have sacrificed their lives for centuries to help others even with the promise of potential danger. There are numerous examples of overcoming fear—an endless list of martyrs and saints whose lives are meant to inspire our faith and encourage us to live without fear. One such person who has inspired me personally is Corrie ten Boom.

Corrie's family had a deep and devoted belief that it was the duty of Christians to care for God's people, and *especially* when their lives were in danger. They put this belief into action during World War II when the ten Boom home became a hiding place for many Jews needing refuge from Nazis in Holland. Eventually the ten Boom refuge was discovered; the family was arrested and sent to concentration camps. When Corrie's father was asked by his captors if he knew he could die for helping Jews, he replied, "It would be an honor to give my life for God's ancient people."* Ten days after the arrest, he died. Corrie lost her father, sister, and brother to the evils of the Nazi concentration camps, but their efforts kept many Jews alive.

It's difficult for me to fathom the faith it took to face such fear and opposition and yet still choose to carry out the mission like the ten Booms did.

The world looks a bit different today than it did in the early centuries of the first church or even during World War II, but the need is the same. Refugees from all over the world are seeking safety and solace from their war-ravaged nations. It's scary to think of taking all of these people in with fear that some may not have good intentions toward Christians—and perhaps this is truer than we realize. Yet I can't help but wonder what incredible stories will come out about the twenty-first-century Christians who recognize the responsibility to care for others no matter the threat or fear.

I'm working on being less scared and more willing to run into the unsafe, unfamiliar, and uncomfortable places that God is asking me to. That's why I'm happy to announce that I haven't backed into any other roommates' cars trying to escape their contagious sickness. Baby steps.

---

* Sophie McDonald, "When Fears Come True: The Corrie Ten Boom Story," *Real Truth Matters*, March 10, 2016, http://www.realtruthmatters.com/blog/when-fears -come-true-the-corrie-ten-boom-story/.

CHAPTER 10

The Language of Your Heart

Nor can there be authentic dialogue unless we are capable of opening our minds and hearts, in empathy and sincere receptivity, to those with whom we speak.

—POPE FRANCIS

On the first day of my high school Spanish class, we were assigned a Spanish name. This name was to be the only one we were allowed to be referred to as long as we were in class. The name I was given was Olga. I thought that Olga would have been a more appropriate name if I were learning Swedish or Russian. I guess in my mind, I was more of a Sophia, Isabella, or Maria kind of girl, but my teacher saw fit to name me Olga. My disdain for my Spanish name should have been an omen for me trying to learn Spanish.

My Spanish teacher was also the girls' softball coach at my high school, and I was on the basketball team. I don't know whether my teacher was partial to the student athletes in his class, but I certainly do not know how I passed that class.

Oh, wait, yes I do.

My mom.

My mom is 100 percent the reason I passed freshman Spanish.

Like so many other high school students, I forgot about my school projects until the night before they were due, and it was usually around eleven o'clock at night that I had this revelation. So the night I remembered I had to make and bring a piñata to Spanish class the next day was no different. I was frantic and stressed, not because I had forgotten the assignment but because the assignment required some artistic ability, and I have none. I am not a creative person. I *buy* presents for friends and I bring store-bought desserts to parties. So making a piñata was not something I could do; buying a piñata at a local party store was. But my teacher had strongly warned against this option and said that if we did bring a store-bought piñata, we would fail the assignment.

Feeling overwhelmed and afraid to fail my class, my mom did what great moms do: she told me to go to bed and she would take care of it. My mom ran to the store to buy balloons and load up on newspapers, crepe paper, glue, and paint. This was long before you could Google everything and get detailed instructions on how to make a piñata. Somehow my mom just intuitively knew. She pulled an all-nighter and saved the day.

When I woke the next morning, I walked into the kitchen to a mess of newspapers, paste, orange crepe paper, and a completed piñata. My mom had made a basketball piñata for me, which was fitting since I was a basketball player and my teacher loved sports. The basketball piñata was not entirely round like a ball at all, but it was orange and had the appropriate black seams. I proudly walked that basketball piñata to class that day and got an A (well, my mom got an A). I hope this confession doesn't retroactively flunk me from freshman Spanish, because there is no way I could pass that class again.

In all, I took nearly four years of Spanish between high school and college, and the best I can do is: *Hola! Cómo está usted? Muy bien, gracias.* I'm pretty sure we learned these phrases the first week of class, and after that, not a whole lot more stuck.

In college, I took another Spanish class, and my professor encouraged us to visit a Spanish-speaking country for an extended period of time so we could get better acquainted with the language. I never did, and my Spanish-speaking abilities suffered. I could read and understand Spanish more than I could speak it, and that was enough to get a decent grade. My professor never really knew how poor my oral language skills were until the end of the semester, when we had to complete an oral exam. Miraculously, I passed each time.

In seminary, I studied Greek and Hebrew. You think Spanish is tough? Try Hebrew. The sounds of the Hebrew language are guttural and not natural for this English-speaking girl from Idaho. And you read backward in Hebrew, which is confusing to me.

Greek, however, is my favorite. I get Greek. It's a language that makes sense to me and is much easier to pronounce. I'm not fluent in Greek yet, but I would love to be one day. I would also love to be fluent in French because I think it is the most beautiful language. But so far I can only remember to say, "*Je veux un pain au chocolat*" (because who doesn't need a chocolate croissant?).

I've heard it said that once you dream in another language, you know you have become fluent in it. We don't have to think about dreaming; we just dream. It is the overflow of our thoughts, ideas, and language. We can't conjure up dreams. They simply come from the abundance of our heart (or from the greasy pizza and scary movie we watched right before we went to bed).

The Bible says, "A good person out of the good treasure of his heart produces good and an evil person out of his evil treasure produces evil, *for out of the abundance of the heart his mouth speaks*" (Luke 6:45).

Another place in Scripture where we see the overflow of our hearts coming through (whether good or bad) is in Matthew 12:34: "You Brood of vipers!" First, I'm going to start using "you brood of vipers" when I really need to get my point across to someone. Too much? Not showing empathy? You're right. Back to the Scripture. "Brood of vipers! How can you speak good, when you are evil? *For out of the abundance of the heart the mouth speaks*" (Matthew 12:34, emphasis mine).

The Greek word found here in both Matthew and Luke

for abundance means "that which fills the heart." Whatever comes from my mouth, or *that which fills my heart*, is abundance. As I read this, I had to ask myself what fills my heart. Just like dreaming in another language comes from a natural overflow of learning, speaking, and surrounding myself by that language, so are my words and actions toward others a natural overflow from my everyday life.

Is my heart full and overflowing with God's love and grace, which spills out with the best in mind for others, or does it secretly hope to see someone fail? Does my heart bubble up with good things to say and actions toward others, or do I always feel inconvenienced when someone around me needs my tender care?

You can't fake what is truly in your heart. We try to fake our real feelings for others by pretending to be happy for them when they get a promotion while we're still waiting for ours. Or pretending to be excited for the woman who got engaged when you're still waiting for a boyfriend. You can't fake *fake*. If it's there, it will come out. It's the language of your heart. There's no way I could fake speaking Spanish. I could try for a second, but everyone would see right through it. But English just rolls off the tongue for me, so there's no need to fake that.

What language does your heart speak in? The one everyone hears and knows? The one that rolls right off your tongue?

How we treat one another is the true language of our heart. Anyone can learn to say the right thing, but we know that actions often speak louder than words. Furthermore, kids can even trick us by saying the right thing just to stay out of trouble. You can't hide your true language. It naturally comes out through your actions.

Regenerate Heart

Several years ago, my neck and back were causing me quite a bit of pain and discomfort, so I went to a chiropractor. I have gone to chiropractors most of my adult life, but I had recently moved to Los Angeles and had to find a new one. I believe that there are ways of healing other than the medical model. The holistic doctor I had been seeing for years heard I was moving and referred me to a holistic chiropractor in the Los Angeles area.

The chiropractor was located in Pacific Palisades right across the street from the beach, and I lived in West LA. In miles, it wasn't that far, but in time, it was a lifetime. After fighting traffic, crazy drivers, arriving late, and the anxiety of going somewhere alone that I had never been to before, I finally arrived. The office smelled like vitamins, and the greeting was less than welcoming.

After filling out the endless paperwork (Am I buying a house?) I finally meet the chiropractor. He sits me down; talks a mile a minute using terminology I don't know, do not understand, and will never understand; and then he feels my neck, my head, and my back. He does dozens of movement and mobility tests and then asks me, "Were you in an accident?"

I don't get white coat syndrome where my blood pressure goes through the roof whenever I see a doctor, but I do get "dumb girl syndrome." It's when a doctor asks you a very simple question that requires a very simple answer and your mind goes completely blank. I guess I panic and think I'm back in school and somehow my answer is graded.

Finally, my brain and my mouth connected and I was able to stammer out, "I don't think so." Pretty sure I'd know if I had been in a terrible accident, right?

The chiropractor went on to tell me I show signs of trauma in my skull and neck. In fact, he tells me that the discs in my neck are degenerating and I have arthritis in my neck. I don't think I spoke again for the rest of the appointment. He adjusted my neck and back and said I needed to come back regularly so that more degeneration wouldn't occur.

I walked out the door and never returned.

I didn't want to believe what he told me. My neck is fine. I just needed an adjustment. I don't have arthritis. I don't even remember an accident or incident that would have caused this. This is ridiculous.

A few years later, the problem was back and worse than ever. I went to see another chiropractor, and this time he took x-rays and asked me the same question the Pacific Palisades chiropractor had asked me: "Were you in an accident?" Once again, my brain and my mouth lost momentary function, and I sat there silent until I finally uttered, "Not that I know of."

The x-rays on my neck proved what two chiropractors were now telling me: my neck was messed up and I needed help. I started getting regular adjustments until I felt better, and then I went on my merry way.

Another year later, not only was my neck bothering me but my entire back became painful. I went to another chiropractor to figure out what was wrong, and for the third time, with a second set of x-rays, from three different chiropractors, I heard the same thing: something was wrong: *You have degeneration in your neck and spine that is causing this pain.* And each doctor reaffirmed the same thing by reminding me I was too young to have this much damage already. Awesome. As if I wasn't already feeling terrible enough, they let me know it was unusual for someone my age. (Way to kick someone when they're already down.)

A degenerative condition occurs when the discs between the vertebrae begin to narrow and wear down, and eventually this process leads to irreversible damage. This, just as it sounds, causes a lot of pain and discomfort. If you don't stop the degenerative process, eventually you will be left with bone on bone along your spine. Eight of the twenty-three discs in my spine had started this process. The only way to deal with the pain was to address the damage.

To this day, I have no idea what I did to my neck and back to cause the discs to degenerate. The only solution was to stop the destruction in its tracks.

The process to stop the discs from decaying any more was intense. I began a three-month program of regular chiropractic adjustments, physical therapy, home care exercises, and tons and tons of icing. The program is designed to do three things: eliminate the pain, stop any more decaying of the discs, and retrain the body to move correctly. It's one thing to accomplish pain management, but the goal is to learn how to stop reinjuring the spine.

As I was going through this process, I kept pondering the word *regeneration*. My doctor made it clear that the degeneration that occurred in my spine can never regenerate. In other words, it can't go back to perfect ever again. I can only stop more degeneration and damage from occurring.

Thank goodness, that is not true for the human heart. Our hearts can be made new again no matter what injury they have incurred that has caused degeneration: selfishness, pride, rebellion, or unforgiveness.

I heard a sermon at a time that my heart had become rather hard toward others. I was still hurting from the loss of Tennyson, and whenever anything in my life didn't work out the way I wanted it to, my heart would grow a little harder. I watched as seemingly everyone else got married and started having families while I was still in the same place I felt I had always been: alone. It was as if everyone else's life got to change with their seasons, but I felt as though I was living a perpetual Groundhog Day nightmare. I would meet someone new, it wouldn't work out, and I was alone again. My friend would meet someone and get engaged in months. I would meet another guy: it would seem promising, and then nothing. Meanwhile, the child I once babysat for asked me to attend her bridal shower. With each new disappointment, my heart grew harder. My heart had been injured, and I had no idea how much it was decaying.

The following Sunday, the preacher read Ezekiel 36:26, and I knew it was especially for me:

> *And I will give you a new heart, and a new spirit I will put within you. And I will remove the heart of stone from your flesh and give you a heart of flesh.* (Ezekiel 36:26 ESV)

A *heart of stone* here in Ezekiel is a stubborn, selfish, and immovable heart. It's a heart that is not teachable or receptive to God's Word of truth or the correction (I know we aren't comfortable with this word, but it's a word we must all learn to embrace) from those around you. If someone (no matter who that person is or what level of influence she has) cannot receive correction and is unwilling to change, it is symptomatic of a stony heart.

My heart was unregenerate. I needed a new heart. My words toward others had become less genuine and not so kind. My actions for others had become callous and unwilling. I needed a new heart.

A *heart of flesh,* as you can imagine, is quite different from a stony heart. A heart of flesh is soft and pliable. It's sensitive to the voice of God and even to those around you.

But most important, it is a heart that is willing to change and open to loving and helping anyone around you.

The crazy thing about my neck and back pain is that I still have no idea what injury caused the degenerative process in my spine. Most likely, I was injured sometime during the years I was playing sports and played through it. I never addressed the injury and probably reinjured it numerous times until the pain was uncomfortable.

It seems that all too often, injuries to our heart go undiagnosed for years. Something terrible happens to us, and we play through the pain. We just keep going through the motions. We continue to act as if nothing is wrong until, over time, that injured heart keeps getting reinjured and all of a sudden our heart has become stony, unwilling, and unreceptive.

We don't care about others.

We don't have the time to help them because, after all, where were they when we needed help?

We don't have kind words of encouragement for someone, since no one encouraged us when we were down.

We walk past, over, and around people due to our decaying heart.

The damage that has occurred in our hearts limits us, causes pain, and keeps us from living the life God has designed us for.

Pain can be catastrophic and can cause the worst to come out of us. We get irritated, lash out, complain, and use choice words. Don't believe me? Ask a friend to drop a hammer on your toe when you least expect it and then see what comes out of you.

The language of our heart as we experience pain is not the language we want the world to hear. Empathy can't survive in a decaying, stony heart. In order to speak the language of love that transcends all cultures and barriers, we must first deal with our own hard hearts.

I could easily have continued pain management for my spine on the road of least resistance with a few pain meds and occasional chiropractic adjustments and let the damage remain, or even grow worse. Or I could take the problem more seriously and commit to stopping the damage once and for all. My choice was to address the problem and stop any more damage. I wish I could tell you that a week later, I was completely fine and pain free. Quite the contrary: the pain got a whole lot worse before it got better. Through the process of trying to get my spine back to where it was supposed to be, the ongoing adjustments and exercises made me feel awful. I had headaches, neck aches, backaches, and pretty much aches everywhere. I wanted to quit. My neck and back had actually felt better before I started all this nonsense. But I remembered that's why I quit all those other times before: the healing process hurt.

Whenever you have to correct something, there's always some pain and discomfort for a while. I was used to my spine being out of alignment, so when we worked to get it properly aligned, it didn't feel so good. Isn't that just like our heart? After I prayed that Sunday for God to exchange my stony heart for a soft heart, it wasn't easy. My heart wanted to go back to its hard, decaying state every time something painful happened. It felt easier to live with the pain than to face it and deal with it. But I stuck with the program, and both my neck and heart stopped gravitating back toward the pain.

God knows the pain you have experienced and the injury you have endured. In fact, he knows it better than anyone (even better than you). He hasn't forgotten you or gone off and left you to fend for yourself. In Psalms, David reminds us that God is near to us in our fractured state.

The Lord is near to the brokenhearted and saves the crushed in spirit. (Psalm 43:18)

David knows a thing or two about a broken heart. Sometimes he caused it, and sometimes he was the sufferer. But in any case, he found that God was close by and ready to put David's life back together again.

God, more than you or me, desires to give us brand-new hearts—hearts that are soft and eager to love, to repent, to forgive, and to empathize with others.

This is the place where we will flourish! We must exchange our beaten, broken, and bruised heart for a brandnew, regenerated heart. When a heart is full of love for God and others, we will find that empathy flows easily and steadily from this renewed heart.

Lean into the Moment

The first time I saw the Eiffel Tower, I was on a boat tour on the Seine looking at all the historic and beautiful structures along the river. I was listening to the tour guide point out and describe all the buildings, when all of a sudden we rounded a bend, and there it was: the most magnificent structure I had ever laid eyes on. It was late in the evening, and I was weary from travel, but the light beaming from the Eiffel Tower gave me life and nudged me from my jet-lagged stupor.

And then it happened—a moment I will never forget. As if the Eiffel Tower wasn't already the most spectacular thing I had ever seen with its bright lights piercing my soul, the tower's lights began to twinkle. The sounds of surprise burst from the other tourists visiting from all over the world, including a loud and giddy "wow" from me. I had seen hundreds, if not thousands, of images and videos of the Eiffel Tower before, but I had no idea that its lights changed from steady to twinkling.

A few years later, I visited Paris again. This time I knew the tower's secret, and I was prepared. I had calculated and was prepared to see the tower light up the sky and twinkle. Once again on my first night in Paris, I went on the boat tour, and as we rounded the bend, just as I had a few years earlier, there it was, the magnificent Eiffel Tower. As we heard the tour guide describe in three different languages Monsieur Eiffel's vision for the structure and the general information about its construction and important dates (all the same information I had heard before), something seemed different for me this time: it didn't twinkle. The sun had just set, and the lights had just illuminated the tower. I kept waiting and waiting for the twinkles to come and for the excited shouts to erupt, but they didn't. Finally, I asked the tour guide when the lights would twinkle. Apparently the tower lights up as it gets dark and then, beginning at 10:00 p.m., it twinkles every hour on the hour for five minutes. We were an hour too early for the show.

I loved that first moment seeing the Eiffel Tower illuminate and twinkle, and everything in me wanted to experience that first moment again. The problem is that we can't experience a "first" more than once. We often try to re-create a special moment from the past, but no matter how hard we try, we can't. We get only one first opportunity. I will have only one first of seeing the Eiffel Tower light up and twinkle. Every time I get to see it again will be glorious, but it will never be like the first time. Our culture loves firsts. We reminisce about a first date or first kiss. We record a child's first words and first steps. Yet we don't seem to get as excited about our first opportunities to meet someone else's needs or our first opportunity to meet a neighbor.

We have only one first opportunity to love someone who is hurting. We get only one shot at comforting someone in the midst of a tragedy. But far too often, we recognize the importance of a first opportunity after the moment has passed. The goal of every Jesus follower should be never to miss the firsts; in fact, we should be looking for them. They are the moments to comfort the broken and the beaten. The moments to generously give to the hurting and remember the forgotten. The moments to love and care for the one who never loved or cared for you. We may be given new and other opportunities and moments, but we'll never have the same first moment again.

I'll never get to see the Eiffel Tower for the first time again, so I'm grateful I lived and leaned into that moment. I soaked it up. Took pictures. Made memories. I want this to be said of my entire life and all the moments that make up my life and story—that I'm present, that I'm aware of the moment, that I discern what is happening, that I see the bigger picture of what God is doing, and that I do what God has called me to do: love others, just as God so graciously loves me.

The Language of Mission

I am obsessed with convenience.

I'm pretty convinced the world's greatest invention is not electricity, the telephone, or even the television. The greatest invention in my mind is the drive-through. I love drive-throughs! Drive-through anything! They are a wonderfully fantastic gift to all of us convenience-obsessed humans.

Growing up in Idaho must have created this intense passion for convenience that I have because drive-throughs are everywhere there. I never knew what it was like to have to go inside to get coffee or pick up prescriptions and dry cleaning or take a check inside a bank to have it deposited—because all of those places were drive-throughs in my neck of the woods. In fact, Boise was one of the first cities in America to have a drive-through Starbucks. Besides potatoes and our blue football turf, this is Idaho's other claim to fame.

When I moved to Los Angeles, I noticed right away that there weren't very many drive-throughs in my neighborhood. I couldn't even find a drive-through bank nearby, and I thought those were standard everywhere. But I finally found the nearest drive-through Starbucks to me. I stumbled on it one afternoon while running errands and couldn't believe my eyes. It was like an oasis in the midst of the desert. I was so elated, I wasted an Instagram post on my Starbucks' drive-through discovery. It was actually nowhere near my house, but you better believe I drove those extra miles, passing several walk-in Starbucks along the way, to get my morning buzz. I never had to worry about getting ready—I could just roll out of bed with no makeup and crazy hair and not worry about a thing because wearing sunglasses in a drive-through makes it all better.

And guess what I saw near my house yesterday? A drive-through Starbucks is being built right around the corner from me. Clearly God loves me and hears my prayers.

Due to my incessant need for convenience I have recently developed an appreciation for Chipotle. I have never really liked Chipotle that much (sorry, Chipotle people); I have always preferred other fast food Mexican restaurants instead. But convenience wins again because there is now a Chipotle near my house, and I have already been there five times and it's only been open for two weeks. Although I don't like it all that much, I'd rather go there and grab a chicken salad when I don't feel like making dinner (which is every night).

Unfortunately for me and for those of you who are honest, convenience isn't always an option in life. In fact, it's rarely the option for a Jesus follower.

I wonder if this is because we all have work to do.

God gives us a job to do, and sometimes it cuts into our own preferences, routines, and agendas. It's simply not very convenient.

Showing empathy isn't convenient. But neither are the throes of tragedy and pain.

Showing empathy is saying that your hurtful circumstances are more important than the inconvenience it causes me. Meeting someone else's needs means not meeting your own.

Christianity is not a system of ethics. We don't love our neighbor, care for the homeless, forgive those who hurt us, or comfort the widow to follow some ethical code. We do it because it is who we are as Jesus followers. We do it because our old self-centered life was crucified with Christ. We do it because we have a job to do.

This is the language of the mission field. The word

mission comes from the Latin word that means "to send." There is a sending that happens when you truly encounter God. Men and women of the Bible would meet God, and then he'd send them on a mission—he'd assign a vocation, a job to do, for his purposes.

This is true from the very beginning: the Creation. God made humans and then gave a job description: "Be fruitful and multiply and fill the earth and subdue it" (Genesis 1:28). I'm pretty sure that is the greatest job description of all time.

God speaks to Abraham and gives him a big job:

> *Go from your country and your kindred and your father's house to the land that I will show you. And I will make of you a great nation, and I will bless you and make your name great, so that you will be a blessing.* (Genesis 12:1–2)

Abraham had to leave his home and everything that was familiar to him. But he did it. He had a mission from God.

Then we read in Exodus 3 how Moses encounters God in a burning bush. God tells Moses to go back to Egypt, where he is from, and rescue the children of Israel. Clearly this was not convenient for Moses because he rattles off to God an extensive list of why he can't or shouldn't go—but God doesn't relent, and Moses goes.

The prophet Isaiah "saw the Lord sitting upon a throne, high and lifted up; and the train of his robe filled the temple" (Isaiah 6:1). After Isaiah encountered the holiness and beauty of God, he asked for a volunteer to go and be a voice to the people. Isaiah's love for God was so great, he didn't delay; he said, "Here am I! Send me" (Isaiah 6:8).

Another example is when Peter became one of Jesus' disciples. In the Gospel of Luke, Peter was out fishing all night and caught nothing. The next morning, he meets Jesus and hears Jesus preach. When Jesus concludes his sermon, he turns to Peter and instructs him to cast his fishing nets on the other side of the boat. Peter was sure that this was a terrible suggestion—he'd fished all night and caught nothing—but he obliges and casts his nets just as Jesus instructed. The nets are now bursting with fish, breaking the nets. Peter, completely humbled and in awe of Jesus, says, "Depart from me, for I am a sinful man" (Luke 5:8).

Peter didn't hesitate to meet Jesus and get a new job. His new mission wasn't to be a fisher of fish but a fisher of men.

We learned earlier while looking at the parable of the Good Samaritan what it means to be a neighbor. Jesus referred to the Great Commandment of loving God and loving others and showed us that the most unlikely candidate of the story was the one who showed love and mercy. Jesus concludes his parable with these words: "You go, and do likewise" (Luke 10:37). We have a job to do: help the hurting and love them toward Jesus.

And then there is the Great Commission. These are the famous last words of Jesus in Matthew's Gospel:

Go therefore and make disciples of all nations, baptizing them in the name of the Father and of the Son and of the Holy Spirit, teaching them to observe all that I have commanded you. And behold, I am with you always, to the end of the age. (Matthew 28:19–20, emphasis mine)

The language of mission is clear to those who follow God. It speaks to us about a calling, a vocation, and a job we have to do. God is asking us to do one thing: *go*. *Go* be a neighbor. *Go* find the hurting and broken and care for them. Be kind and compassionate. Put others first. Be inconvenienced. Be available. Listen to understand. Forgive someone who doesn't deserve it. Lose yourself. Cry with, laugh with, and be with the people God places in front of you. Surprise the world with empathy!

I believe the job God has given each of us is the mission of showing empathy.

We want healing in our relationships. We want miracles in our world. But we don't practice empathy.

We want a miracle in our marriage, but we refuse to listen to our spouse's perspective. Instead, we view everything he says through the lens of what he hasn't done right. We set him up to fail.

We want to heal from the racial tension that is saturating our nation, but we don't want to listen to generational stories or upsetting statistics. We don't want to hear what we don't want to believe. We don't want to listen to the painful cultural memory that lies deep in the social fabric of our country. We ignore the reality of those suffering from injustice, because we don't look through the lens of empathy.

Empathy is not limited to our preferences. God is for the powerless and the powerful. He is for the marginalized and the privileged. God's love cascades down to everyone. No one gets excluded from God's world of empathy. So we must not be selective in our practice of empathy.

I don't believe we will see the healing and miracles we desire until we first have empathy. We have to start listening to understand a different perspective. Then we must pray that God will help us see what we cannot see naturally or on our own. And then, I believe, miracles will happen in our homes, families, communities, and entire world.

It all starts with empathy.

ACKNOWLEDGMENTS

Mom, Dad, Krist, Rachelle, Mark, Kelly, Kenzington, Westley, Quincey, Whitney, and Chloe—you are my heart and you all deserve my greatest gratitude for your constant love and support. Mom, thank you for always cheering me on, endlessly praying for our family, and for all the times you acted as my "personal assistant"—you deserve a raise for this unpaid job! Dad, thank you for teaching me to selflessly love and serve others as I've watched you live it out. Krist, we all know you're the smartest—everything I know, I've learned from you. Thank you for letting me talk to you for hours about this project, bouncing thoughts off your genius brain, and asking you a million questions. You are my hero! Rachelle, you are my first and forever best friend. Thank you for always being there for me no matter what—whether to encourage or defend. You always have my back. Mark and

Kelly—I couldn't have handpicked better spouses for my siblings! Love you both and so thankful we're family. Kenzie, thank you for being patient with your aunt TT throughout the writing of this book. Now we can have all those sleepovers and dates you have been asking for!

McCarty family, Brian and Marchelle, Jim and Eli, and Bryan and Diane, thank you for sharing a portion of Tennyson's life with me. I pray this book would encourage many lives and bring comfort to those hurting from loss—may this be a tiny part of Tennyson's great legacy he left behind.

Capital Church—thank you for always loving me, praying for me, and supporting me. I'm so grateful you are the church that raised me and for all the incredible lifelong friendships that have come from my wonderful church family. Love you all dearly!

The City Church LA—thank you for allowing me to be a part of your story. You will always have a piece of my heart!

Esther and Whitney—thank you for believing in me and working so diligently (meanwhile, having fun together and laughing along the way). You two exude the strength, confidence, and grace that every woman who leads should have. Love all my Fedd Agency ladies!

Lauren—only you could make being locked in a room writing for days so much fun. Thank you for polishing my words and making sense of my heart on paper. You are gifted beyond your years and I am honored to have your input and help on this project.

The Team at Howard Books—thank you for embracing

the message of this book and for taking a chance on me! All of your devotion to this project was above and beyond!

Lisa—I knew from our first conversation that this book was always meant to be in your caring hands. Thank you for cherishing the message and allowing me to tell my story—and thank you for teaching me so much about empathy through yours.

And above all, Jesus. You are my forever and always.